A YEAR IN
THE WILDERNESS

A YEAR IN THE WILDERNESS

Bearing Witness in the   Boundary Waters

Amy and Dave Freeman

MILKWEED EDITIONS

Published 2017 by Milkweed Editions
Printed in Canada
Cover and interior design by Mary Austin Speaker
Typeset by Mary Austin Speaker in Wilke LT
Cover photo by Nate Ptacek
Author photo by Nate Ptacek
All photos by Amy and Dave Freeman except the following:
Ron Doctor: 11; Nate Ptacek: 19, 24, 111, 136, 138, 208, 211, 228, 219, 223;
Ellie Siler: 36, 292; Michelle Hesterberg: 293
17 18 19 20 21 5 4 3 2
First Edition

Milkweed Editions, an independent nonprofit publisher, gratefully acknowledges
sustaining support from the Jerome Foundation; the Lindquist & Vennum Foundation;
the McKnight Foundation; the National Endowment for the Arts; the Target Foundation;
and other generous contributions from foundations, corporations, and individuals. Also,
this activity is made possible by the voters of Minnesota through a Minnesota State Arts
Board Operating Support grant, thanks to a legislative appropriation from the arts and
cultural heritage fund, and a grant from the Wells Fargo Foundation. For a full listing of
Milkweed Editions' supporters, please visit milkweed.org.

Library of Congress Cataloging-in-Publication Data has been applied for.

Milkweed Editions is committed to ecological stewardship. We strive to align
our book production practices with this principle, and to reduce the impact of our
operations in the environment. We are a member of the Green Press Initiative, a
nonprofit coalition of publishers, manufacturers, and authors working to protect the
world's endangered forests and conserve natural resources. *A Year in the Wilderness*
was printed on FSC certified sustainably forested paper by Friesens Corporation.

*We dedicate this book to Joseph Goldstein
and all the folks speaking loudly for this quiet place.*

CONTENTS

"Wilderness can be appreciated only by contrast, and solitude understood only when we have been without it. We cannot separate ourselves from society, comradeship, sharing, and love. Unless we can contribute something from wilderness experience, derive some solace or peace to share with others, then the real purpose is defeated."
—SIGURD F. OLSON

"Wilderness can change who we are for the better, but it can't protect itself—it relies on us to understand its importance in our lives and guard it for the future."
—JOSEPH GOLDSTEIN

"Wilderness is not a luxury but a necessity of the human spirit."
—EDWARD ABBEY

A YEAR IN
THE WILDERNESS

BEGINNING

It was 11:00 p.m. on September 22, 2015, and we were busy sifting through the boxes of food and piles of gear strewn across our pre-expedition headquarters in a friend's home near Ely, Minnesota. Inside, the pine floors creaked and groaned. Outside, the moonlit silhouettes of black spruces through the window were a reminder of where we would soon be spending an entire year. At that moment we were just ten miles south of the Canadian border and only a couple miles from the next day's destination: the Boundary Waters Canoe Area Wilderness, a roadless, million-acre maze of forests, lakes, wetlands, and rivers.

As we moved from pile to pile, worries and questions churned through our restless minds. Are we packing enough food? Should we bring two or three folding solar panels? Which charging cables do we need—and why does every electronic device seem to require a different one? Did we update all of our automatic bill payments and provide a forwarding address for our mail? Will our parents be able to get a message to us if Grandma gets sick? How are we going to file our taxes in April? And—perhaps above all—why are we worrying about laptops, digital cameras, and a satellite terminal before heading off on a canoe trip?

Weeks of frantic planning, organizing, and packing had led up to what was, for us, entirely familiar—piling food and gear into a canoe and paddling into the wilderness. We tried to tell ourselves that we had done this hundreds of times before and that the following day would be no different: we would load the canoe, zip up our life jackets, hop in, and paddle away. But of course it would be different. In the morning there would be TV cameras and reporters. If all went as planned, a flotilla of canoes, pontoon boats, kayaks, and paddleboards would escort us to the Wilderness boundary, and we wouldn't follow them out—much less lie in a bed, flip a light switch, or flush a toilet—until the earth had completed one full rotation around the sun.

Slowly the items we would need during each season found homes in fourteen plastic bins stacked along the wall, waiting to be neatly labeled. The electronics might have seemed the most daunting and out of place on such a journey, but they were quite possibly the most important pieces of equipment we would carry.

THAT HAD BEEN true on our first big adventure together, too. When we kayaked around Lake Superior nearly a decade ago, our giant camera—twice the size of the one we packed now, with a telephoto lens—was always accessible, wedged in one of our cockpits. Back in 2002 Dave had cofounded the Wilderness Classroom Organization, a program that connects elementary and middle-school students with explorers. Circumnavigating Lake Superior was the ninth Wilderness Classroom "learning adventure." Throughout our journey we would make good use of our technology to share photos, scientific data, blog posts, lesson plans, and other educational materials with five thousand students from across the country through WildernessClassroom.org.

On the eve of that trip, in late August 2006, the surf pounded the pebble beach outside Superior Coastal Sports in Grand Marais, as we went through much the same packing exercise, if on a smaller scale, in an apartment upstairs. More than a thousand miles of rugged, storm-battered coastline lay ahead of us. Many people had warned us that September and October were too stormy and that we would be stuck for days or weeks

Our last morning kayaking around Superior

waiting out storms. They were right. It was hard. It was cold. We were windbound for a total of seventeen days, huddled in our tent, listening to the surf hammer the shore, wondering when Gichigami would let us move on. Between the storms we often paddled from dawn until dusk, arms aching and minds in a trance from the endless repetition.

But as we learned, long journeys are addictive. They distill life down to its most basic essence, hone your mind and body, fill your soul with energy and confidence. We made it back to Grand Marais fifty-seven days later. When we woke up that last morning, our spray skirts were so stiff that we had to thaw them on our laps for an hour before we could put them on. Water droplets froze to our life jackets, kayaks, and hair as we paddled the final seventeen miles. But when we pulled our kayaks up onto the pebble beach where we had launched nearly two months before, we were grinning from ear to ear, feeling like we could accomplish anything and knowing that we were stronger and happier as a team. We had learned that embracing the challenges and discomforts

This storm pinned us down for four days

Peruvian children watch Amy answer students' questions

of wilderness travel is part of what makes us feel alive.

After such a rewarding journey, we were excited to continue sharing our expeditions with classrooms. We just needed to figure out what to explore next.

WE FINISHED SIFTING through the bin of batteries and charging cables. As always, the familiar motion of closing the crush-proof dry box's lid and the reassuring click of its big yellow latches reminded us of previous adventures. No doubt some of

the case's scratches still held traces of the Amazon's silt, picked up during a six-month, three-thousand-mile journey across South America by bicycle and canoe in 2007 and 2008. Then the case had protected our electronics from the Amazon's torrential rains and muddy banks by day, and had provided a seat in the evenings, when we might convene by candlelight in a palm-thatched hut, a gaggle of wide-eyed village kids peering over our shoulders as we answered questions sent by students across the United States.

The dry box slid neatly into the bottom of our green equipment pack, nestled between sleeping pads and sleeping bags. Many years ago we learned to pack in reverse order so the things we would want first when setting up camp on a cold, wet, dark night would be immediately accessible. With this in mind, we added the tent, stakes, guy-lines, and tarp, all waiting for our first campsite in the Boundary Waters, somewhere along the Kawishiwi River. The tent was new, its olive fabric still shiny and crisp, but as we cinched the pack closed we talked about the tent we were leaving behind. That yellow

dome tent was one of our most-used wedding presents—though after sheltering us for more than 700 nights under the stars, it was not up for another 365 nights in the wilderness.

We had set it up for the first time a month after we were married, in the temperate rainforest of the Pacific Northwest. During that first night of our honeymoon, a torrential rain drummed on the nylon. The next morning we would leave Bellingham, Washington, for a three-year, 11,700-mile journey by kayak, canoe, and dogsled across the

This tent was our primary home in the Wilderness

continent—an expedition we called the North American Odyssey. That tent sheltered us from many storms as we traveled to Arctic Canada and then to Key West.

We turned our attention from the equipment pack to attach canvas bags to our two toboggans, before rolling them up and securing them with rope. Suddenly eleven-foot sleds were transformed into compact bundles that could easily be stored until they were brought into the Boundary Waters for the winter, where they would be pulled by three borrowed sled dogs. The scene transported us back to the winters of the North American Odyssey, when a Dene elder in a remote community in northern Canada told us that when you travel by dog team you see every rock and every tree—and the land speaks to you. His people couldn't hear the land anymore, he said. They had traded their dogsleds and canoes for trucks, snowmobiles, and satellite TV. The elder's words had stayed with us. A connection with the land has to be cultivated and cared for. At the most basic level, we entered the wilderness to listen to it.

-40° in the Northwest Territories, Canada

Canoe paddles leaned against the wall next to our pack, each dent in their wooden shafts and chip in their carbon fiber blades telling the story of all the places they had taken us. They had propelled us through some of North and South America's most stunning wilderness—and had even brought us home to Ely in fall 2011, in the middle of the North American Odyssey. By that point we had spent eighteen months traveling seven thousand miles. Millions of paddle strokes had formed substantial calluses on our hands and our bodies were hardened by the work.

That stop at home was strategic. We would spend the winter leading dogsledding trips for Paul and Sue Schurke's Wintergreen Dogsled Lodge, to help refill our depleted bank accounts. In the spring we would continue our journey across the Great Lakes, through the Saint Lawrence Seaway, and eventually down the East Coast to Key West. But it was an accidentally life-changing stop as well. Humpback whales approaching our kayaks, caribou streaming across frozen lakes, and a forest fire engulfing the shoreline in hundred-foot flames—these were all images that left lasting impressions on us. But our human interactions during the journey

were what would eventually lead us to the edge of the Boundary Waters.

That winter we heard the first rumblings about proposed copper mines near Ely. Iron-ore mining had been going on in the region for generations, so at first we didn't think these new proposals would be much different from what was happening already on the Iron Range. We weren't activists: we had signed our fair share of online petitions, but we were not participating members of environmental groups; we voted, but had never called an elected official or written a letter to a government agency. The more we learned about the long history of pollution and the unique risks associated with sulfide-ore copper mining, however, the more concerned we became.

We were wilderness guides and educators, and viewed our role in environmental protection as enabling people to experience the wilderness, fostering a love and appreciation for the natural world. Our work shifted with the seasons. For many summers we had led canoe trips in the Boundary Waters and sea kayak adventures on Lake Superior. When the water turned to ice we harnessed dog teams for expeditions outside Ely. The wonder

Kayaking with humpback whales in Alaska

and personal growth of our clients were constant reminders of the value of wild places. That was what had motivated us. But then fate—in the form of Frank Moe—stepped in.

Frank had represented the Bemidji area in the Minnesota legislature for several terms before he and his wife, Sherri, moved to a tiny cabin outside Grand Marais to devote more time to racing their sled dogs. In March 2012 Frank was planning to deliver thousands of petitions from northern Minnesotans opposed to sulfide-ore copper mining to the governor, Mark Dayton, a project Frank called Sled Dogs to Saint Paul. If all went as

planned, it would take him a week to mush the five hundred miles south. But Frank needed another dog team to meet him in the town of Finland with a set of petitions from Ely, which he would add to his load.

After we met Frank for coffee, we agreed to deliver the petitions. This task took us out of our comfort zone—we were nervous about rocking the boat—but our jobs and way of life depended on these lakes and rivers, and it seemed like everywhere we had gone on this trip and others the land was being cut, used, abused, and silenced. We couldn't help but remember the smell of

Kayaking on Lake Superior

smoke and ash amidst the abundance of the Amazon, as we paddled past thousands of acres of freshly cut and burned rainforest. We have paddled through Superfund sites—and a massive blue-green algae bloom on Lake Winnipeg that gave the water the consistency of pea soup and made it unsafe for even our dog to drink. We once set up camp on a beach in British Columbia piled so high with trash washed in from the ocean, we spent five minutes clearing plastic bottles, shoes, fishing nets, and hunks of styrofoam just to accommodate our tent. There was enough plastic to fill a barge. We felt helpless; there was no way we could transport it all in our tiny kayaks. There was much we did not yet feel equipped to do. We could drive a dog team, though, so we did.

Six weeks later, in May 2012, we loaded our kayaks on the cobble beach in Grand Portage, ready to resume our journey across North America. Students from the local school came to see us off, and an Anishinaabe man gave us a small pouch of tobacco and encouraged us to leave offerings in the waters that lay before us. We would travel over

four thousand miles in the next eleven months. Twelve hundred hours of paddling—about four million paddle strokes—offered plenty of time for us to reflect on the lessons of the winter, and to think about the value of clean water and of wild spaces like the Boundary Waters. We were proud of the work we had done, but it wasn't enough. We didn't really know what we could or would do, but as we migrated south along the East Coast at twenty miles a day, our conversations centered more and more on the joys of our own experience, joys we wished everyone could take part in: the water we could drink right out of the lakes and the vast public lands where we could pitch our tent unhindered by "no trespassing" signs.

Finally the noses of our kayaks touched the white beach in Key West. It was a little anticlimatic. Amy's parents were running a few minutes late, so our welcoming party consisted of a security guard who told us that kayakers were not allowed to land on that part of the beach. It didn't matter; we still hugged and took our photos and felt like we could do anything we set our minds to. And then, after four years of focusing on this

landing, we were left with the liberating yet daunting task of finding a new path forward.

THE SMALL POUCH of tobacco we were given in Grand Portage stayed with us long after Key West. It would accompany us during our year in the Boundary Waters too. In our pre-expedition headquarters we tucked it in the outer pocket of our equipment pack for easy access, to serve as offerings to the land and water we were about to explore.

We grabbed our faded life jackets from a bin and set them near the pile of essential items that we would start our journey with. We had been offered new ones, but we turned them down. The familiarity of these jackets hugging our bodies brought us comfort. After all, they had traveled thousands of miles on our torsos.

Two months after we reached Key West, in June 2013, we walked into Sustainable Ely, an old house that was being established as an education and action center aimed at stopping the proposed sulfide-ore copper mines along the southern edge of

Paddling the Inside Passage

the Boundary Waters. Volunteers were painting the walls, dropping off furniture, and staffing the front desk. Sitting on sawhorses was a shiny new canoe with a few dozen signatures dotting its tan hull. As we browsed land-use maps and informational handouts, we asked about it. The woman behind the desk excitedly explained that they were going to cover the canoe in signatures from thousands of people who opposed the proposed mining and then they were going to drive the canoe to Washington, DC, and deliver it to President Obama. We signed the canoe and a seed was planted.

A week before visiting Sustainable Ely, we had purchased an old twenty-seven-foot sailboat from a friend. We planned to spend the summer guiding, learning to sail, and living on the boat in the Grand Marais harbor. After three years living out of our tent, we couldn't bear the thought of a house that didn't move, and even the smallest of conventional homes seemed cavernous and intimidating. For twenty-seven hundred dollars we had a tiny floating house that, with a little elbow grease and practice, could take us anywhere.

In the V-berth of this new home a few nights later, our conversation turned from strategies for eradicating the sailboat's black mold to Sustainable Ely. We had a strong desire to get involved and help protect a place that we care about and that has given us so much. Canoes are meant to be paddled: what if we took the canoe to DC by water? The idea began to grow and by the end of the summer the wheels for our next expedition were in motion.

The first step was to convince Becky Rom. We had never met her before and really had no idea who she was. But we did know that the canoe belonged to Northeastern Minnesotans for Wilderness and that Becky was on their board. She grew up in Ely and her father Bill Rom was good friends with author and conservationist Sigurd Olson. This was fortuitous. To the conservationists who knew Sigurd Olson, he was a visionary; to those in favor of development in the Quetico-Superior (in the form of logging, mining, or even landing floatplanes), he was a formidable adversary. To us, he is best described as a conservation hero and role model.

As teenagers, our concept of wilderness had been shaped by his words. But his conservation legacy extended much farther than his eight books (of which *The Singing Wilderness* is the most well-known). In addition to his local work, he served as wilderness ecologist for the Isaak Walton League, president of the National Parks Association, president of the Wilderness Society, advisor to the National Park Service, and advisor to the Secretary of the Interior. He helped draft the Wilderness Act of 1964, which created the Boundary Waters Canoe Area and established the US wilderness preservation system. As kids, though, we just knew that his words painted a picture of the landscape we yearned to explore. Reading Sigurd Olson's books allowed us both to bide our time in high school in Saint Paul, Minnesota and Western Springs, Illinois. Appropriately, the canoe itself was named Sig, for two reasons. One: in honor of *Sig*urd Olson. Two: because people were putting their *sig*natures on it.

Becky was impressive herself. From a young age she had worked to protect the Boundary Waters. She became a lawyer, served on the board of the Wilderness Society and other organizations working to protect public lands, and was now leading the fight to protect the Boundary Waters from the mines. We would

Visiting the Washington Monument with Sig

need her backing and the unflinching support of Sustainable Ely's growing network of volunteers and concerned citizens to have a chance to make a difference. The physical part of the trip was relatively simple: compared to some of our other expeditions this was a straightforward journey, and we had already paddled much of the route on the North American Odyssey. What we didn't know how to do, and could not do on our own, was develop and implement a strategy for using Paddle to DC as a tool for grassroots activism.

Sitting on the lawn behind Sustainable Ely one summer day in 2013, Becky laid out both the history of the conflict and the strategy for stopping the mines. Ely and many of the surrounding small towns, she told us, sprang up after iron ore was discovered in the region. Becky's grandfather worked for the Pioneer Iron Mine, which operated from 1888 to 1967, closing when Becky was in high school. Over time Ely's economy shifted from a mining and logging emphasis to a tourism-based one, heavily tied to the Boundary Waters.

In the 1960s International Nickel Company (INCO) discovered copper just south of the Wilderness boundary, near the South Kawishiwi River and Birch Lake. They purchased two mineral leases from the federal government and took hundreds of core samples but then copper prices tanked. The leases changed hands and were renewed several times, but no mine was ever built. In 2011 Twin Metals Minnesota began a feasibility study to look at mining these old leases, and in 2012 they submitted an application to renew the leases for the third time.

Becky and a handful of other lawyers had looked at the lease agreement and determined that the federal government was not required to automatically renew. And they encouraged the federal government to assess the impacts of mining on the edge of the Boundary Waters—something that had not been done to begin with—before moving ahead. Becky believed that an environmental review would establish the edge of our nation's most popular wilderness area as an inappropriate place for an industry the Environmental Protection Agency has identified as particularly inclined to pollution.

Sulfide-ore copper mining is very different from—and much more environmentally dangerous than—iron-ore mines like the one Becky's grandfather worked in. There are more Superfund sites in the United States from this type of mining than from any other source. And every place sulfide-ore mining has been done worldwide has suffered from significant ground or surface water pollution. The main problem, Becky told us, lies with the massive amounts of waste rock produced by this form of mining. Copper, nickel, and other minerals sought make up less than 1 percent of the ore pulled from the ground. But all the ore is crushed in order to extract the minerals, and that powder contains small amounts of sulfide—thus, sulfide-ore mining. Mix air and water with that waste rock and you get sulfuric acid, which is essentially battery acid. The mine might be open for a few decades, but the millions of tons of waste rock could leach mercury, lead, arsenic, and other toxins into the environment for centuries.

In Sustainable Ely's backyard, Becky used rocks to pin down maps showing mineral deposits, hydrology, and federal leases. As we pored over these maps, as well as scientific reports and Twin Metals' own documents, our hearts

sank. The facts were unavoidable: a multibillion-dollar international mining giant was looking to build an enormous industrial mine complex at the edge of the Boundary Waters Canoe Area Wilderness, in the middle of the Superior National Forest, which contains 20 percent of all the freshwater in our National Forest system. The water, lacking natural sources of carbonate, has very little inherent buffering capacity. Any pollution would be very hard to mitigate.

How could two people, a canoe, and a handful of volunteers possibly top a giant international company and its big-money lobbyists? On the other hand, what choice did we have? We knew full well that doing nothing would likely lead to the development of a massive industrial mining zone, damaging this maze of lakes and rivers that is central to our very being.

Luckily, our idea complemented Becky's vision. She saw paddling to DC as a catalyst that could help build a national movement to protect the Boundary Waters, amassing a coalition of millions of people—business owners, hunters, anglers, conservationists, veterans—here in Minnesota and across the nation.

MAPS HAVE BEEN a constant in our lives together. In Ely we sifted through our collection, pulling out the maps we would need during our first two weeks. Tattered corners, countless creases, streaks of mud and grime, and our handmade marks for favorite campsites and closely guarded fishing holes flooded us with memories. In the Boundary Waters we were returning to a place we knew, a place where we felt entirely at home, if only we could make it through those final few hours of sleep-deprived chaos.

During Paddle to DC we discovered how precious the Boundary Waters is not just to us, but to Americans from all corners of our nation. We learned that when we stand up for what we believe in, we can anticipate being joined by others, who speak collectively in ways that are infinitely more powerful than a single person's voice or actions. Though we were physically alone, pulling with our paddles toward DC at three miles an hour, we were part of a growing movement. Over the next 101 days,

Paddle to DC send-off outside Ely

nearly a hundred radio, television, and newspaper stories about Paddle to DC gained a lot of attention for the cause. Meanwhile the Campaign to Save the Boundary Waters had grown from one part-time staff member and an intern at the beginning of our journey to a rapidly growing full-time staff with offices in Ely, Duluth, and Minneapolis, as well as a team of pro bono lawyers in DC, by the time we reached its end. And a wave of people following our journey were also calling their representatives, signing petitions, donating, volunteering, and taking millions of other individual actions to help protect the Boundary Waters.

That kind of momentum was electrifying, even when experienced from our vantage point in the canoe. The idea of spending a full year in the Boundary Waters had been floating in our minds for many years, but until Paddle to DC it was a distant dream, something we would do after we started to slow down, perhaps in retirement. But as we paddled toward the Capitol, we began thinking of a year in the Boundary Waters as a continuation of our efforts. The first step, though, would be planning—and in the short term we would need to refill our bank accounts. Just a week after

arriving in DC, we were scheduled to guide our first dogsledding trips of the season back in the Boundary Waters.

The first nine months of 2015 were a whirlwind of guiding, presentations about Paddle to DC, and preparing for A Year in the Wilderness. Finding support can be as demanding as any other challenge we undertake. To help keep the cost down, most of our clothing and equipment, and a significant portion of our food, was donated by companies and individuals who care deeply about the Boundary Waters. This was a huge help, but building those partnerships required many phone calls and emails. We also partnered with the Campaign to Save the Boundary Waters to write grants and raise funds. Their staff spent countless days crafting marketing materials and media plans, organizing resupplies, soliciting volunteers, and helping to ensure we made as big an impact as possible before, during, and after the expedition. Between meetings, phone calls, and guiding trips we were busy dehydrating fruits and vegetables, compiling food and gear lists, and hunkered down in front of our computers doing everything else required to plan A Year in the Wilderness.

WE WERE MAKING progress in our pre-expedition headquarters. A strong gust of wind outside reminded us to check on our canoe. We had sanded and teak-oiled its gunwales earlier in the day. Now they were dry, so we flipped the canoe over to prevent the wind from disturbing it and returned inside.

The piles were getting smaller, but we were exhausted. Simple decisions—will we want one or two new pairs of socks in January?—were getting harder and harder to decipher. It was time to sleep, something we had not done for more than a couple hours each night for the previous several days.

It was 2:00 a.m. when we climbed into our soft bed. But sleep did not come quickly. We would have to get up in a couple of hours to whittle away at a to-do list that seemed to get longer as the hour of our departure grew closer. Trying to anticipate every item or piece of information we would require for an entire year was no easy task. We still needed to download books to our Kindle,

update the apps on our iPad, and compile and share passwords and instructions with the folks who would be helping us update websites and social media accounts, pay our bills, and otherwise run our lives outside the Boundary Waters. But the biggest job that remained was carefully inventorying each piece of equipment so that it could be brought to us by friends and volunteers throughout the year.

It felt like our brains were buzzing with electric pulses of light when we closed our eyes and tried to clear our minds. We were too tired to think, but the endless stream of calculations and unanswered questions removed any hope of meaningful rest. Two pounds of granola, two pounds of oatmeal, one pound of coffee, one box of chocolate cake mix, half a pound of milk powder . . . would this food last for the two weeks until our first resupply? How many bags of tea would we want? Was six pounds of trail mix enough? Would we get sick of rice and lentils or spaghetti as our only dinner options? *Don't forget to pack the tomato sauce powder that just arrived in the mail. . . .* What

Dried food that would turn into a feast

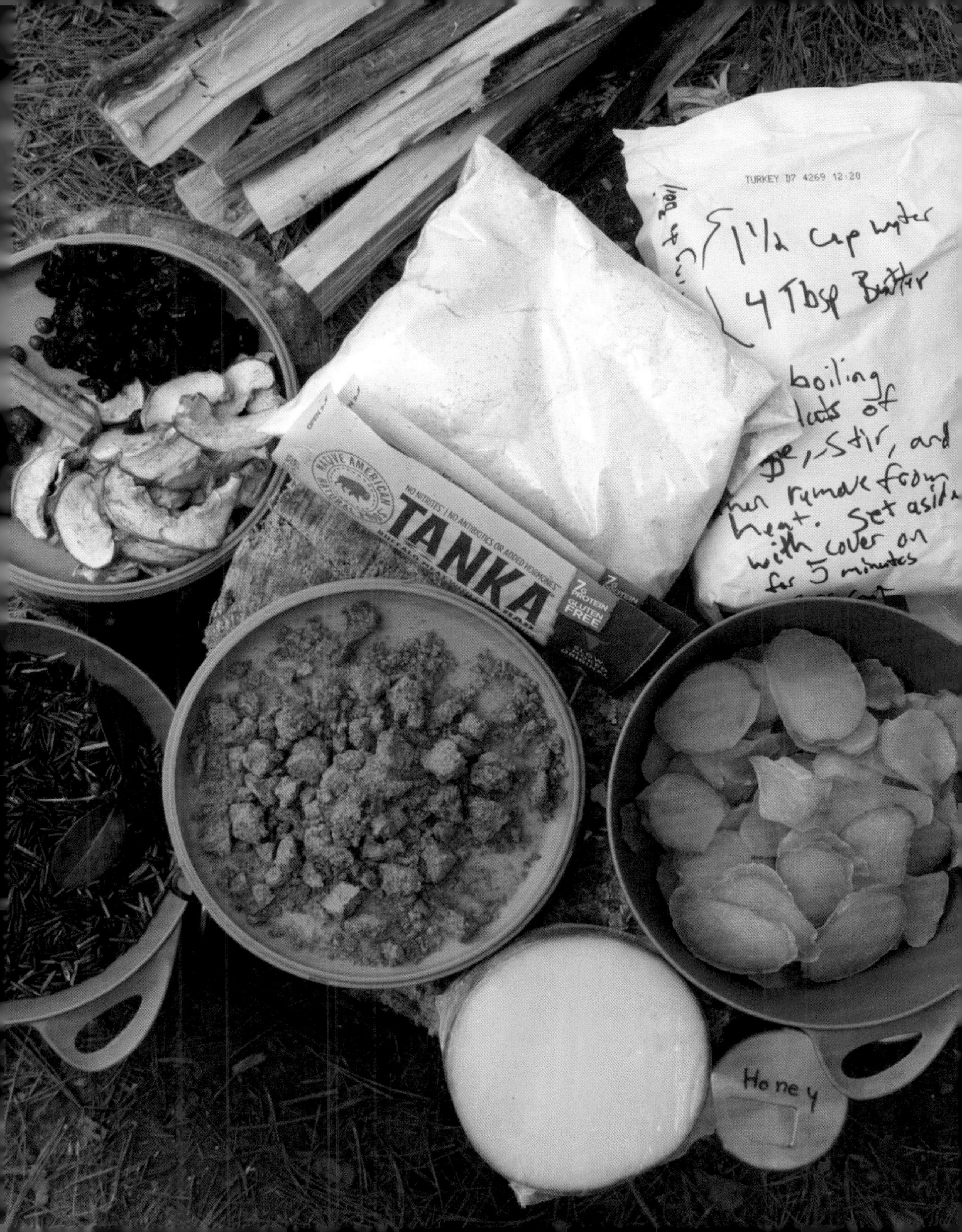

TURKEY D7 4269 12:20
1 1/2 cup water
4 Tbsp Butter
boiling
lots of
Stir, and
remove from
heat. Set aside
with cover on
for 5 minutes
NO NITRITES | NO ANTIBIOTICS OR ADDED HORMONES
TANKA
7g PROTEIN
GLUTEN FREE
Honey

if we felt trapped and wanted to leave the wilderness after a month or six months? What if this extended Boundary Waters experiment started wearing on our relationship and forced us apart? What if one or both of us was counting the days, hours, and minutes until we could take a shower or return to the modern world? What if our cameras broke or we couldn't get the satellite terminal to work? We had already spent too many precious hours both on the phone with tech support and huddled at a picnic table in downtown Ely, trying to get our satellite terminal to work in the rain. After days of trial and error we finally had to mail the terminal back to the factory for repairs, less than twenty-four hours before paddling into the Wilderness. Our goal of sharing daily photos on social media, writing regular blog posts, recording a weekly podcast, and conducting interviews from deep inside the Boundary Waters seemed to be disintegrating before we even took our first paddle strokes or captured the first image.

What if people forgot about us? What if our goal of using this year as a tool to advocate for the protection of the Boundary Waters fell on deaf ears? More than anything this last thought gripped our minds, making it exceedingly difficult to take advantage of our final night on a queen mattress layered with blankets and cozy flannel sheets.

We knew we could do this; the bugs, cold, rain, portages, slush, and sore muscles were all minor discomforts we had learned to accept and, at times, even relish. We had both been drawn to the wilderness since we were kids. Over time and many adventures our skills had been honed. With that had come the knowledge that even the longest portages eventually end, that a breeze would provide temporary relief from the mosquitoes when we thought we could not stand them any longer, and that we would set up camp after it felt impossible to take another step or paddle another stroke, only to feel refreshed as the sun's first rays heated the tent the next morning. More than anything we just wanted to be on the water, gliding across a lake toward our first campsite, knowing that the silence and simplicity there would soothe our frazzled brains.

We had been in that place many times before, perched on the knife's edge between adventure and chaos. As we finally drifted off, we took comfort in remembering that many of the same worries had filled our brains on the eve of other expeditions. In the end we were never going to be 100 percent ready. We just had to do our best and then trust each other. Figuring out far-off details like how we would file our taxes from a remote corner of the woods would have to wait.

IT WAS 7:00 a.m. on September 23, the fall equinox, and the alarm was sounding. We rubbed the sleep from our eyes and we each took a long shower, relishing the hot water, the lovely scent of shampoo and soap. Our last showers, we thought mournfully. For a year.

In the kitchen, steaming plates of spinach-and-sausage quiche served by our host and friend Jason Zabokrtsky, owner of Ely Outfitting Company and Boundary Waters Guide Service, momentarily replaced our checklists. As we relished the warm cheesy dish, Jason noted that this would probably be our last quiche for the foreseeable future. We had noticed this tendency in ourselves—and others—to point out what we would be missing. But would we really feel deprived of

modern conveniences, we wondered, when surrounded by natural beauty?

A year's worth of camping gear spilled out of the plastic bins, and piles of packs, clothing, and food lay in a semiorganized pattern in the center of the room. Rich black coffee brought us to life as we imposed order on these remaining items. It was comforting to know the first of two dozen resupplies would be brought in by volunteers in just a couple weeks. If we forgot something, it wouldn't be the end of the world. A whole network of people had our backs.

With three hours to go we shuttled the gear bins to our year's headquarters at Sustainable Ely, and puzzled over how to wedge four apples, a head of cabbage, three tomatoes, and a fresh loaf of bread into the top of our food barrel without squishing them. Two weeks' worth of food just fit in the barrel. It took both of us to get it to the car for the drive to River Point Resort on Birch Lake, a short paddle from the Wilderness boundary. We slid fishing poles, life jackets, and our day pack into the car as well and tied the canoe on top.

The list of things left undone would have to wait. Inertia pushed us forward, along with the knowledge that we were part of something much bigger than just the two of us. Our expedition manager, Levi Lexvold, handed us sandwiches as we climbed into the car; his simple act of kindness reminded us that we were not alone. As we prepared to leave Ely, we thought of the words of Sigurd Olson: "When we talk about intangible values remember that they cannot be separated from the others. The conservation of waters, forests, soils, and wildlife are all involved with the conservation of the human spirit. The goal we all strive toward is happiness, contentment, the dignity of the individual, and the good life. This goal will elude us forever if we forget the importance of the intangibles." These intangible values bring us all together in common humanity. Friends and strangers alike wanted us to succeed, not just in spending a year in the Boundary Waters, but in protecting it for future generations.

All we could do then was close the car door, leave civilization behind, and let the adventure begin.

Clear Lake sunset

FALL

We arrived at River Point Resort in the midst of a downpour. The owners—Steve and Jane Koschak, and their son, James—momentarily stopped setting up tents and tables to greet us. With a big grin, Steve told us that he had checked the radar, and optimistically declared that the rain would be over by the time folks started arriving.

While the Koschaks finished their preparations, we unloaded the canoe and gear and set our packs under the awning of the fish-cleaning shed. The packs would soon be exposed to all kinds of weather, but we could not shake the instinct to keep them dry just a little longer. We left our two blue barrels by the canoe, raindrops richocheting off their impervious lids.

A few minutes later Steve and Jane asked us to follow them out to a rocky point. There we found a sunflower, a couple of feet high and in full bloom, facing the lake. Its yellow petals and green stem were bright against the steel-gray water. Steve said it was a good omen; we chose to agree, though we secretly wondered if it had been planted for our benefit. Regardless, it made us smile. We spent a quiet moment there, grateful for the sunflower and for the clean water beyond. The distant call of a loon brought us back to the present. The rain had stopped.

Waving goodbye to the flotilla

FRIENDS, FAMILY, WELL-WISHERS, and local TV news crews arrived in small groups, and soon there were nearly a hundred people talking, celebrating, and carrying canoes down to Birch Lake. After everyone had their fill of the Koschaks' coffee, cider, and pulled-pork sandwiches, the crowd gathered at the waterfront and we slid our canoe into the water. We paddled a few yards offshore and waited for the flotilla to join us, our nervousness subsided with each gentle wave.

We headed northeast, surrounded by friendly chatter and song. But at the Highway 1 bridge the flotilla stopped, and our canoe crossed under its shadow alone. We turned to wave before continuing on against the current of the South Kawishiwi River. Slowly the sounds of motors and human voices were replaced with those of the wind in tree branches and our paddle strokes.

Over the next two hours, we settled into a rhythm of portaging and paddling. Halfway through the fourth portage, we crossed the Wilderness boundary. A couple bald eagles perched high atop a dead white pine coolly observed us as we paddled out.

Eagle soaring over the Kawishiwi River

We picked up our pace in the final mile of the day as the sun dipped lower in the sky. Though we were rusty, we managed to pitch the tent and cook dinner efficiently enough to get in bed before dark. Just as we zipped into our sleeping bags, the patter of drops on the tent began. The sound built in strength and intensity as a steady rain drenched the forest around us. We were lulled to sleep by its calming rhythm, grateful to be warm, full, and dry.

We spent the next day in camp, acclimatizing to the forest and recovering from the frantic pace of the days preceding our departure. At one point, a high-pitched cry from the lake brought us running. We saw an osprey plummet from the sky, rippling the water's dark surface with its talons as it snatched a fish. And yet a low hum of machinery—either logging activity just outside the Boundary Waters, or traffic on Highway 1—was audible. The faint, unnatural sound reminded us that we were not there just to admire the area's beauty, but to protect it.

AS THE DAYS grew shorter and the leaves turned vibrant, we settled into a routine of camping and paddling. We remained in familiar territory, base-camping for several days at a time, but excursions to nearby lakes, rivers, and streams allowed us to gather water-quality data for the Minnesota Pollution Control Agency and samples for Adventure Scientists' microplastics study. After paddling to the deepest point of a lake, we would lower a probe and note the dissolved-oxygen levels and temperature at each meter descending from the surface to the bottom. We used a secchi disk to measure the lake's turbidity, and another pocket-sized device to measure its conductivity.

Several days after we had entered the Wilderness, Steve Piragis casually paddled up to our site. A biologist by training, he too collected data in the Boundary Waters, in the 1970s. It was what had first brought him to the region and how he had met his wife, Nancy, before they opened an outfitting business and store in Ely.

Steve was the first of some three hundred visitors we had throughout the year. We depended on these connections to receive food and swap out gear roughly every other week. The resupplies enabled us to travel in a manner similar to most paddling and dogsledding visitors to the Boundary Waters. Steve was keen to see our tipi-style tent and collapsible wood stove. After we gave him a tour, he hopped in our canoe and we made our way to Bruin and Little Gabbro Lakes for a day of exploration.

While we portaged, Steve taught us about mushrooms. Most of the leaves had already fallen off the underbrush and the mushrooms were easy to spot emerging from the duff on the forest floor. Walking through the woods, our footsteps stirred up the damp leaves on the trail and the scents of earth and decay were rich. From dangerously lethal (death angel) to hallucinogenic (fly amanita) to edible (puffballs and lobster), we saw a good sampling of the fungi of the northwoods. Fascinated by the lobster mushroom—an unappetizing morsel made tasty when infected by another fungus—we carried a

softball-sized chunk back to camp at the end of the day, with instructions from Steve to sauté it with our dinner. He retrieved his canoe and we were alone again.

AS WE MOVED from camp to camp, our bodies gradually grew accustomed to the motions of packing, paddling, portaging, and setting up once more. Each day began in the tent, as we stuffed our sleeping bags into sacks and rolled up our pads. Then one of us emptied and packed the tent while the other began boiling water from the lake. The cool air had formed beads of condensation on the outer surface of the tent, causing fingers to sting while packing it. Breakfast and coffee would be ready by the time everything other than the cook kit was packed. After finishing our oatmeal, we carried our packs down to the water's edge and carefully lowered the canoe into the lake. One of us held the canoe as it floated parallel to shore and the other loaded it.

Later that day we settled into a

Preparing to camp on Thomas Lake

new home with a south-facing granite shore. We basked on the sloping pink rock, then went for a chilly swim. We left our solar panels lying on the rock, taking advantage of the first sunny day since we set out. As the droplets of water evaporated off our skin, our anxieties and concerns of the past week dissipated in a similar manner. We still hadn't worked through all the logistics, lists, and what-ifs, but being in the wilderness had somehow made them less significant. In just a few days, shelter, warmth, and companionship had taken priority over emails, fundraising, and conference calls.

Two loons, an adult and a juvenile, circled the glassy lake as the sun set and the nearly full moon rose. We sat silently on the rock, watching and listening. As they drifted past, one whistled softly. Was the juvenile seeking comfort from its mother? Or was the adult reassuringly cooing to its young? We went to bed that night thinking about the loons. The air temperature and water were getting cooler every day. When would they fly south? Was the little one big enough to make the journey to the Gulf of Mexico?

We would miss the birds' haunting calls when the last of them left the Boundary Waters for the winter.

IN EARLY OCTOBER, waking up to frost in the mornings became a common occurrence. An evening fire in the woodstove became a necessity rather than a luxury, so gathering, cutting, and splitting firewood were added to our camp chores. By the end of each day, our shoulders ached and we slept deeply.

Following the Isabella and Perent Rivers took us into an area that had been ravaged by the massive Pagami Creek Wildfire four years earlier. We paddled through a landscape of charred tree trunks, exposed gabbro, and dense scrubby underbrush. Initially we felt bewildered and sad for the loss of this forest, but we soon began to appreciate the stark beauty. The fall foliage was not in the treetops where one would expect, but the rugged ground was covered with a waist-high sea of gold and deep red-brown, under colorless trunks rising to the sky.

Trees charred by the Pagami Creek Wildfire

On Bald Eagle Lake we camped near the mouth of the Isabella River and quickly learned that it was a haven for migratory waterfowl. Each evening we heard skeins of Canada geese gliding overhead and then landing at the river mouth. Each morning we woke up to their cacophonous honking. The chatter would reach a crescendo and all their wings would start flapping. Once they took to the air, one goose would utter a few more emphatic honks, and they'd be gone.

The forest was filled with the energy of animals on the move or frantically preparing for the winter. Mushrooms appeared in odd places, like the branches of a fir or spruce at eye level or even a fire grate, stashed by squirrels as if on a pantry shelf above their anticipated snow level. This energy was contagious. We had been the bearers of it ourselves on past journeys, as we neared the end of a route in late fall, trying to get somewhere before freeze-up. Not now. We would keep moving, but we did not have a destination we needed to reach. We would discover answers to questions we had always wondered about. When would the last loons leave? Were the bears already hibernating? When would the ice begin to form? How would our own bodies adapt to the cooling air?

One morning we sat in a campsite on Lake One, facing a golden hillside striped with the barren trunks of burned trees. Fog slowly burned off as the sun rose in the sky. Suddenly we heard a rush of air and looked up to see a bald eagle swoop down and land on a rock just offshore. Seconds later a mink scampered past the eagle. The slender creature shook water off its coat, briefly illuminating it in a halo of light. Had the eagle disturbed the mink from its perch? Or had the eagle carried the mink to this spot— playing with its food? The eagle remained stoic and still as the mink darted into a crevice.

This campsite had been like an office of sorts to us, as we spent several days using our devices to post photos and text online. But now it was time to leave, so we loaded our canoe, warming our hands after dropping each pack in the hull, and then shoved off. The heat of the sun increased with each passing

Floating across Vera Lake's glassy surface

minute. Along shore we spotted a male moose, camouflaged in the tan grasses but exposed by the absence of mature trees. As he turned to head inland, his sleek dark coat gave way to pale hindquarters, where he had lost hair trying to rub off unrelenting ticks.

The weather turned unseasonably balmy that day and we took full advantage of it by paddling until sunset. The western horizon glowed orange and pink as the inky purple of night rose up out of the east. With only the dark outlines of rocks and trees visible, we continued on, content to set up the tent in the beams of our headlamps. As we did so, a pair of glowing eyes startled us before we saw the white feet that went with them. It was a snowshoe hare, already changing color despite the lack of snow on the ground.

WE WERE NOT entirely alone in the wilderness, of course. We had already met new people by coincidence and by their own intention, as they monitored our trip on the Internet. But old friends came to us, too. One afternoon in October, fourteen-year-old Joseph Goldstein and his father, Jeff, paddled the cedar-strip canoe they had built together toward our campsite. They were followed by Joseph's younger brother, Jacob, and our good friend Jason, who had hosted us before our departure and was also the Goldsteins' longtime guide.

Joseph was our guest of honor. He and his family had made frequent trips to the Boundary Waters in the summer and winter ever since he was little. Shortly after being diagnosed with leukemia in 2014, he had been given the opportunity to make a wish. He thought on a grand scale: he matter-of-factly said that he wanted to save the Boundary Waters from the threat of proposed copper mines. While the organization offering the wish was perplexed about how to proceed, Jason put Joseph in touch with the Campaign to Save the Boundary Waters.

Joseph came into our lives in November 2014. We were about a week away from completing our journey to Washington, DC. The weather was cold, rainy, and at times snowy; we were traveling through an urban landscape that was entirely foreign to us. We dodged ferries and tankers, and camping became nearly impossible in a land of cement, fences, and private property. But a phone call with Kemia, Joseph's mother, brought tears to our eyes and inspired us to continue on. His voice, we realized, made ours stronger.

On the drive home from DC we stopped at the Goldsteins' house for a brief visit. We gave Joseph one of our paddles. He showed us the cedar strip canoe he and his dad were working on and explained to us that the Boundary Waters was his favorite place in the world; he wanted to help protect it for his little brothers. Before we got back in the car, we knew that we would stay engaged with the cause. And indeed, when Joseph found out about our plans for A Year in the Wilderness, he said he wanted to join us for the entire year, downplaying the importance of his freshman year of high school and ongoing chemotherapy. We offered a compromise: Joseph would come out to see us and deliver a resupply once every season.

Now Joseph's crew was pretty well soaked—especially Jacob, who had fallen in at some point. Our tent was suddenly full of wet socks and polar fleece dangling from drying lines. The next day we departed camp under gray skies. Fueled by Swedish pancakes and propelled by a northwest wind, we made good time heading down the length of Knife Lake, with a brief detour to Isle of Pines. Before the Boundary

Joseph and Jeff Goldstein

Waters gained its wilderness designation, this spot was home to Bill Berglund's Isle of Pines Resort, where Dorothy Molter, a trained nurse from Chicago, came to help out and eventually own the resort. With the passage of the Wilderness Act in 1964, the property was condemned and purchased by the US government, and she was told to leave. Her plight gained national attention and she was allowed to stay—making her the last person to live in the Boundary Waters Canoe Area Wilderness. There she brewed root beer for passing canoeists, and came to be known as Root Beer Lady. After she passed away in 1986, her cabin was relocated to Ely, where it serves today as a museum.

Molter was the last person to call Knife Lake home, but there were many before her. The Anishinaabe called it Mookomaan Zaaga'igan, and the French Canadian voyageurs named it Lac des Couteaux, or Lake of Knives. As the glaciers that carved Knife Lake receded more than ten thousand years ago, Paleo-Indians moved into the area. We paused in a nondescript cove to examine where they quarried siltstone and shaped it into stone tools. After thousands of years we could just imagine what must have been a bustling scene of ancient people flaking knives, axes, and other tools. For hundreds of generations people have lived on this land and traveled these waters, leaving scant clues of their existence or scars behind. Now modern humans wanted to employ massive machines to mine, crush, and haul millions of tons of rock in search of copper along the edge of the Boundary Waters. If a mine were to be built, what scars would remain ten thousand years from now? We pondered this question as Joseph and Jacob climbed out of their canoes to examine the smooth gray rock.

Four days with Joseph and Jacob made us see the Boundary Waters with new eyes. Watching Jacob erupt with wonder every time a fish struck his line and seeing Joseph expertly coax damp wood into a crackling campfire reminded us of trips we had made when we were their age, and of the sense of wonder and accomplishment this wild expanse inspires.

On our final portage together

snowflakes drifted down lazily. The snow increased in intensity throughout the evening and by the next morning the canoes and tents were dusted in white. The morning sun melted the snow before our friends launched their canoes and paddled out of the Boundary Waters.

WE MADE OUR way up the Basswood River alone, portaging around rapids and marveling at the power of the fast-flowing water. A campsite nestled between a set of small rapids beckoned, and we sat on a rock ledge there well past sunset, watching the stars come out and the moon rise behind scraggly oak branches as the constant hum of the tumultuous water reverberated off the rocks.

In the morning we had to decide whether to take a mile-long portage to Basswood Lake or to follow the course of the river. In the end, the river won out. We knew that going this way would take longer, but the desire to see what was around the next bend was a strong motivator.

Portaging along the Basswood River

So we paddled, waded, and portaged along the Basswood River to its source, having given in to the pull of that tumbling, drumming, roaring water.

On Basswood Lake a full moon illuminated our campsite and we stayed up late. Whether the cause was the moon itself or the sounds and energy of all the nearby animals, we couldn't say. Something kept our brains turned on and our senses heightened well into the night. Trumpeter swans made their presence across the bay known through honks and flapping wings. Eager to capture the moment, we grabbed our audio recorder and ran outside just in time to catch several flying over our campsite. The sound of the massive birds' wings would make it into our next podcast, to be saved on a memory card and sent via resupply parties to the producers at WTIP, a community radio station based in Grand Marais. These podcasts served as a way for us to share the sounds of the wilderness.

As we walked back to our tent, it took a minute to locate the source of a new, subtler sound. Crunching. It was coming from the water's edge.

Preparing to paddle at dawn

What would be crunching down there? A series of squeaks gave away the otters feasting on crayfish in the moonlight.

CRUNCHING WAS A sound we would hear more frequently as the weeks passed and the nights grew longer. In the mornings the paddles were encased in hard frost. The marsh grasses and tree branches glistened in the soft light. Our bow broke through a thin layer of skim ice near shore. We experienced the first burn of numb fingers and that familiar sting in the lungs as our heart rates and breathing increased while portaging. Hauling our first load would get the blood flowing and warm our appendages. After a few minutes we would be clawing at zippers and removing hats. By the time we finished a second trip across the portage, we would be down to base layers.

We crunched through more skim ice and wound our way through a surreal landscape as the marsh grasses lining the shore glowed white, blue, and purple with their rapidly melting veneer of frost. A lone gray loon floated on the main

body of the lake, seemingly unfazed by us, busy preening with one foot held in a seemingly impossible position above its body.

As we crested a hill on the portage into Moose Lake we saw two men walking our way. Nate Ptacek and Matty Van Biene would spend a week with us, in the first of three visits to help us document our journey and complete a short film called *Bear Witness*. A serendipitous tweet in 2013 had led to Nate joining and filming us for ten days during Paddle to DC. When we decided to spend a year in the Boundary Waters we immediately reached out to him again—and, working together, we were lucky enough to secure several environmental film grants from Patagonia to fund *Bear Witness*. We paddled and portaged to Basswood Lake as Nate and Matty kept their canoe in sync with ours and filmed.

On Basswood Lake a couple boats glistened in the distance. We knew more friends were out here whitefish netting. As we paddled up, their silhouettes took on the identifying features of our dear friends and fellow dogsled guides Jason, Ellen Root, and Van Conrad. We could hardly contain our excitement at seeing their familiar faces. This was our first time seeing Ellen and Van since we had entered the Boundary Waters, but not our first time in the wilderness together. We spent

three months dogsledding across the Northwest Territories with them in 2011. As we drifted in our respective boats joined by hands clasping gunwales, we fell into easy conversation, as if no time had passed.

We set up camp with the videographers on a campsite two hundred yards away from our friends. It felt good but a little strange to be sharing a campsite with others. For a few days we were part of a small community. We spent time on both campsites, sharing meals and whitefish netting duties—with Nate and Matty filming all the while.

On our first night together we clambered into the frost-covered canoe to paddle back to our campsite. The water was perfectly smooth and a light mist hung just above the surface. It was so cold we could see our breath. Our headlamps illuminated the watery path. The beam of a headlamp penetrated the water and we quickly realized that there was a lot going on below the surface. First one whitefish, then another lazily swam below the bow of our canoe, confirmating that they really did come to this spot to spawn every year. After spending the summer schooled up, feeding on invertebrates near the cold dark bottom

of the deep parts of the lake, they seemed out of place here in the shallows. Triggered by a drop in water temperature, they were in search of relatively shallow water and a gravel bottom. They spawn at night, so although we were marveling at what we saw, we didn't linger for fear of disturbing their private affairs.

A northwest wind kept us landbound except to check the nets in our protected bay. It was a cold, unpleasant task. Untangling the whitefish, bare hands quickly got wet and slimy. We all took turns filleting the fish, using cutting boards balanced on five-gallon buckets. Those who were on a break from filleting rinsed and packed the fish. Once the last fillets were rinsed and packed, relief came to numb fingers in the form of warm wash-water in a bucket.

We ate some of our catch, but most of the fillets were saved to be smoked later. Our connection to the land deepened over those few days spent catching and processing fish. For those few days we ate well and drank a lot of fresh ginger tea in Ellen and Van's warm tent, and caught up on the goings-on in Ely. When their trip was over, it was hard to part. As we found ourselves alone again, we held back tears and got angry with each other over trifling things. Behind us were good friends—and ahead of us was the unknown and potentially dangerous freeze-up.

THE SUN WAS setting by the time we hauled our gear up a steep slippery trail to our campsite, set up the tent, cut and split a evening's worth of firewood, and prepared to cook dinner. The heat tempted us, but the lake's glassy surface beckoned to us as well. We each donned an extra layer and returned to the water. As the sun disappeared below the western horizon, a tinge of orange illuminated the clouds and it became hard to tell where the far shore ended and the lake began.

In the past we had rarely taken the time to watch the light fade and change, let alone head out in a canoe at dusk or dawn to immerse ourselves in it. After almost two months in the Boundary Waters our pace was slowing. We often found ourselves lifting our heads from evening chores, glancing west to note the cloud cover and vantage point, and guessing at the beauty of the sunset. Would a cloudless sky paint the land with the day's last golden rays? Would scattered clouds explode with color after the sun dipped out of sight? Or would a gray day slowly fade to moonless, inky blackness? They all had their merits; we were just glad to have the time to stop and observe this daily cycle.

Floating in the stillness, we marveled at the waves of red and purple washing over the sky and water. There were no sounds: no trees rustling, no gunwales banging, no calls from a distant campfire. In the summer Ensign Lake would have been dotted with campers. But now we were totally alone, with one of the most popular lakes in the Boundary Waters all to ourselves. Winter was coming and the Wilderness would be largely ours for the next six months.

The temperature was dropping and our tent awaited us. But as we pulled our canoe up onshore, a pack of wolves broke the silence with a chorus of howls. Cold fingers and food were instantly forgotten. We

Listening to the wolves on Ensign Lake

scrambled to find our audio recorder. They continued to howl as we frantically attached the microphone and hit the record button. We sat at the water's edge, watching and listening as the last color faded to black. When they quieted we tilted our heads back and howled, but the wolves did not respond. We could hear splashing across the lake, where water flows into Splash Lake. We had noticed a large school of ciscoes preparing to spawn there earlier in the day—were the wolves fishing?

We groped our way back to the tent in the dark. We made our cold fingers locate our headlamps and load the woodstove. Why hadn't we loaded the stove when it was light out and relatively warm? Winter would require greater efficiency. In another month or two 35 degrees would feel balmy; it could easily be 60 or 70 degrees colder come January.

We woke up to the distinctive sound of wet snow hitting the tent. We poked our heads out to find a land covered in white as big puffy flakes streamed down. The forest was entirely silent. We lingered a

few extra minutes in the warm tent. After loading the canoe with stinging hands, we paddled vigorously toward the narrows between Ensign and Splash Lakes. We were eager to get our blood pumping, and curious to see if the wolves had indeed been drawn to the ciscoes.

As we approached the narrows a small gray wolf sprinted up the northern slope. After its initial flight the wolf turned to examine us, cocking its head and sniffing before picking its way up the rocky hillside and disappearing over the ridge. The bow of our canoe touched the moving water and we were swept down the riffles. Two eagles erupted from the rocky bank and landed in a gnarled jack pine overlooking the cisco-filled pool. They peered down, beaks speckled red.

We pulled into the eddy and climbed out of the canoe. From the look of things a feeding frenzy had been underway for some time. The rocks were covered with tiny bloody scales shimmering in the daylight. Hundreds of ciscoes pulsed in and out of the shallow rapids, their ten-inch silver bodies moving in unison. We crouched, watching an ancient

Cisco scales speckled with blood

annual tradition unfold before us—a new generation being deposited in the rocks below. How many ciscoes were spawning in rapids all over the Boundary Waters at this moment? Time seemed irrelevant until the cold seeped through our clothes, urging us on.

Crossing Splash Lake we were immersed in white. Impossibly large snowflakes floated in the still air around us, disappearing into the dark lake but coating the surrounding forest. We tipped back our heads and stuck out our tongues. We were about to meet a group of friends and volunteers for our final resupply before freeze-up and it seemed fitting that they would paddle out in a snowstorm.

Soon we were chatting and stuffing ourselves with doughnuts and hot apple cider on the portage between Splash and Newfound Lakes. They offered us homemade treats and news from near and far. In return we told them about the wolves and ciscoes, the eagles and snowshoe hare, as we rummaged through the treasure trove of food and winter clothing they had hauled in. But they had an eight-mile paddle back

Paddling across Splash Lake in the snow

to their cars and it was cold, though the snow had stopped, so it wasn't long before hugs and handshakes faded into silence.

As the last canoe paddled out of earshot, we considered how best to fit all that we had just acquired into our canoe. Two brimful food barrels, a pack filled with winter clothes and warmer sleeping bags, and snowshoes were a lot of additional cargo. Our nineteen-foot-long canoe was made for carrying a big load, but perhaps we were pushing things a little. Still, we figured, we had fit forty-two days worth of food and gear, as well as a 104-pound sled dog, in this canoe once before. Slowly we wedged our stuff in, leaving just enough room for us.

When we entered the water we were riding an inch or two lower. We initially it felt like we were paddling in quicksand, but once we had some momentum the canoe handled beautifully. Feeling optimistic after the snowfall and the visit, we decided to aim for Knife Lake, five portages away. Getting there before dark was unlikely, but neither of us cared. We dug in with renewed purpose.

When we pulled up to our last portage, a beaver signaled our arrival with a sharp warning slap of its tail against the water. In the dimness we could barely make out the ripples where it dove under. We ate a couple Clif Bars and dug out our headlamps and warm jackets. As we hefted our packs, we knew we were walking in the steps of history, following a path worn by generations of Native people and then European explorers in the 1700s. Our loads were heavy, but thinking of the voyageurs of that period we knew we had nothing to complain about. Our heaviest pack approached ninety pounds; two hundred years ago the voyageurs trotted across this portage carrying two or three ninety-pound bales of furs or trade goods at a time. They would travel by canoe for eighteen hours a day, carrying massive amounts of goods to the far reaches of Canada, where they traded for furs to be made into beaver-felt hats for gentlemen in Boston, London, and Montreal. During the fur trade more than two million beaver pelts were packed across these portages.

Hauling our supplies to Knife Lake

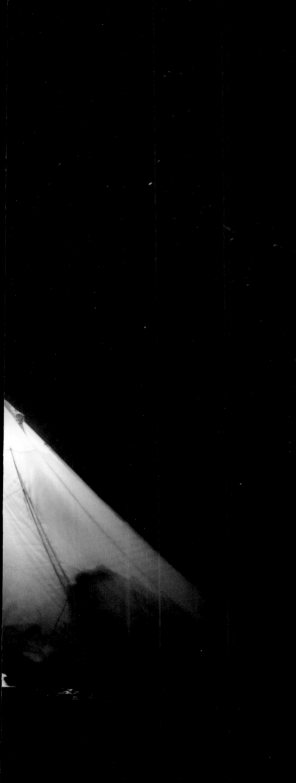

It was pitch black by the time we set our third and final load down at the edge of Knife Lake. We struggled to wedge the snowshoes behind the stern seat before climbing into the canoe. Switching our headlamps off, we paddled into the darkness. Stars shone through the thinning clouds, pinpricks of light dancing on the lake's smooth surface. We felt alive and alone in the Wilderness, melding with the vast universe reflecting off the water. We were so small, seemingly insignificant, here for just a fleeting moment. Purposeful paddle strokes propelled us toward our favorite campsite, tucked in the middle of a peninsula, surrounded by towering red pines.

It was 8:30 by the time we climbed into the tent. As heat radiated into our stiff fingers from the glowing stove, the tent filled with the aroma of stew and damp wool socks. We devoured every last spoonful of stew and licked the pot. Food, water, shelter, companionship—our time in the Wilderness so far had made it apparent to us that these simple things are what really matter.

Cooking dinner under the stars

THOUGH FREEZE-UP HAD not yet come, we found ourselves stranded on Knife Lake. Our new satellite terminal wasn't working. It had been delivered with the last resupply to replace our old terminal that we had mailed to the company shortly before entering the Boundary Waters. Up until this point we had remained relatively close to the periphery of the Wilderness so that we could send updates with a cellular signal on a semiregular basis. Here, if we climbed to the top of a hill, we could still get a weak cell signal. We yearned to head deeper into the Wilderness, but if we couldn't post photos and blog updates, our travels would be pointless. That was, after all, our primary reason for spending the year in the Boundary Waters—to share the experience, to keep the place on people's minds over the course of an entire year and inspire them to do their part to protect it. The invisible umbilical cord of a cell signal kept us tied to this spot. We trekked up and down the hill

for service daily and got to know the satellite tech support by name.

If not for the subtle indicators of changing weather and animal activity, we felt as if we were living the same day repeated. Our resident chipmunk no longer emerged from its underground den once the nights dipped below freezing with regularity. The forest grew quiet, as migrating birds disappeared. Wind blowing through bare branches and the occasional raven or flock of black-capped chickadees were the only sounds to be heard. The few remaining loons had turned gray and no longer yodeled. Ice formed along shore in sheltered bays. Daylight decreased by minutes each day, driving us into the tent to cook dinner and write earlier and earlier. We kept busy by organizing our ample food supply and winter gear, going on multiple firewood gathering missions, and then processing and piling the firewood in our campsite. We charged batteries whenever we could with the diminishing light.

A few snowflakes drifted in the air one evening, causing a gentle tapping that lulled us to sleep. After waking in the diffuse light

Slowing down as the seasons change

of morning, we lay relishing the warmth of a tent that had been insulated by the snow. Emerging from our sleeping bags we triggered an avalanche of heavy snow down the exterior of every wall. By spring this sound would be enough for us to estimate how much snow had fallen overnight as well as its moisture content.

Listening to the radio while cooking dinner had become a habit. If we weren't gathering the "news" of the northwoods, at least we could hear what was going on in the rest of the world. One evening we heard about six attacks in Paris, killing over a hundred people. We were horrified and angered by these senseless acts of violence carried out four thousand miles from our tent under the red pines. We faced very real risks in the Boundary Waters: capsizing our canoe in cold water, running out of food, or falling through the ice. But no threat Mother Nature could throw at us was as frightening as people with automatic weapons randomly killing innocents.

Portaging to Paulson Lake as the sun sets

ONCE THE SATELLITE terminal was functioning we headed east. Snow remained in the shade; on each portage we looked for animal tracks and found those of wolf, fox, and marten. This provided us with a taste of what was to come in the winter. We would know the comings and goings of various animals not by actually seeing them, but by the evidence of their movements recorded in the snow. We briefly met friends and received a few treats from them on Seagull Lake before veering off toward the portage to Paulson Lake. A month would pass before we would see any other people; it would take a while for the significance of this to sink in. From now on our margin of safety would be thinner. After enough ice had built up to prevent travel by canoe but before there was enough to support our weight, we would be entirely dependent on each other. This scared us a little but it also brought smiles to our faces. Being alone out here meant being utterly free.

The sun had already set by the time we completed the rugged one and a half mile portage to Paulson Lake. A chill came on quickly as the

clear sky darkened and our activity level decreased. We choked back an underlying primal sense of panic that stems from exhaustion, hunger, dropping temperatures, and darkness as we set up camp in the narrow beams of our headlamps.

We awoke to a cold gray morning devoid of sound. No chickadees, not even a raven greeted us. We powered on the satellite terminal long enough to send an update and check the weather. The forecast was for consistent temperatures below freezing. If we didn't immediately head back to Knife Lake we risked getting frozen in on one of these remote smaller lakes.

The narrow boggy channel before the main body of Glee Lake was covered in a half inch of ice so our canoe became an icebreaker as our bow cut a path through the ice. We were relieved to see that the ice was thinner on the main body of the lake, invisible until it shattered upon contact and we saw the water displaced by the canoe burbling up through holes. In the thicker ice, we were occasionally taken by surprise as a paddle ricocheted off the surface. We had to forcefully

Breaking ice on the creek into Glee Lake

punch the paddle downward. Our forward momentum came from the pressure of the paddle blade on the ice instead of the water. We poked one hole in the ice at a time, like a climber grabbing hand-holds. Our progress slowed to a crawl, and our stroke placement was made visible by the holes we left behind us. Keeping up momentum was key— the bow rode up on the ice for a few seconds before crashing down through it and settling back afloat. The bow of the canoe cutting through ice created a continuous grinding or glass-breaking sound, jarringly loud, punctuated each time we drove our paddles through the ice. When we did finally hit a patch of open water the quiet was palpable.

From then on we paddled with a new sense of purpose—get back to Knife Lake before we were frozen in. On Fay Lake we trained our eyes on what we assumed was driftwood or the root ball of a downed tree. Then it moved. The moose had been wading in the water, eating aquatic plants, and took off uphill into the burned landscape. Its face was a weathered gray. One ear drooped. How much longer would it be able to wade into

the water? It seemed to have been eating with the same sense of urgency with which we were paddling.

Two long days later we reached Knife Lake and in the simple act of returning to this campsite for a second time we created a semblance of home. A pile of moose droppings on the latrine trail at the top of the hill indicated that at least one creature had passed through in our absence. And so we began the wait for freeze-up on Knife Lake.

A lone loon swam around our little bay in the dark. It had been quite a while since we had seen or heard any, so we had assumed they were all gone for the season. It bobbed its head as it glided through the water. Was it injured? When would it fly south? Perhaps this one traveled here from farther north and was taking a break. Where was its mate? Thinking of this loon all by itself led to unabashed anthropomorphizing on our part and we hugged each other a little tighter, grateful to be in this together.

Temperatures in the single digits at night caused a rim of ice to grow and sing in the nearby bay. Ice makes surprisingly loud sounds as it is forming. Pops, pings, and sighs stood out

Flipping the canoe after a sunset paddle

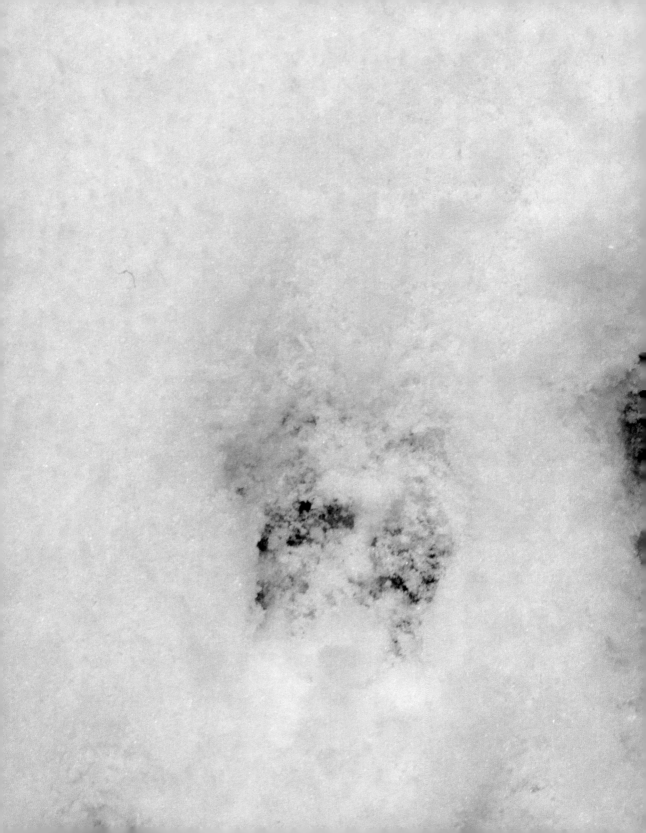

to us at first, but, like many of the natural sounds we had become accustomed to, eventually these too faded into the background of our consciousness. With the lake still mostly clear, we decided to take one last opportunity to gather firewood in the burned area to the northeast. We could also check on the condition of shallow Bonnie Lake.

We donned warm layers, dry suits, and life jackets, knowing full well the danger of cold-water immersion. On the short portage we were the only creatures leaving fresh tracks in the snow—at least until we crossed several little highways covered with tiny rodent footprints, where red-backed voles had emerged from their tunnels in the subnivean layer, scampered across the gap, and reentered the safety of the snowpack on the other side. These small creatures had a whole world that we hardly ever witnessed in the wintertime.

As we crested the last hill we caught a glimpse of a snow-covered lake stretching out before us. We both squealed with excitement. We were anxious to see how thick the ice was, so we gingerly stepped onto it,

Checking the ice on Bonnie Lake

staying near shore. The blade of our axe punched easily through an inch and a half of clear ice, just barely enough to hold our weight. Before heading back to camp, we filled our canoe with some beautifully seasoned, slightly charred wood.

The thickening ice was heartening. The colder the night, the more excited we were; a warm day brought despair and made us question the onset of winter. On one morning paddle, we looped around our little point and were enchanted by Knife Lake's ice-encrusted shoreline. Bulbous icicles hung from rocks and branches. This was the work of the waves generated by days of wind. Slowly, imperceptibly, the repeated splashing of water had built up intricate and amorphous shapes. The ice-coated rocks had become smoother, more artfully rendered versions of their usual rough and jagged selves. Tree branches were encased in ice and drooped with the weight of transparent tentacles. Farther down the lake cliffs lay under bumpy blankets of ice, with occasional stripes of pink or yellow revealing the minerals that continuously seeped from the rock. The

portage to Vera Lake was coated in snow and fresh pine marten tracks led the way. Snow fleas—springtails, actually, out to feast on a fungus in the snow—clustered in sunny spots. Upon closer observation, the tiny black specks were constantly moving, even bouncing. But Vera's ice-free surface disappointed us.

On our paddle back to camp one loon surfaced and we assumed it was the same one we had been seeing. Then another appeared nearby. We were relieved to know that these two loons had each other. Somehow we worried less about a pair than an individual. The similarity of our situation to that of this loon pair made us appreciate each other even more. Neither of us had any desire to be out here by ourselves. Being with one another increased our safety and efficiency, but there was more to it than that—something intangible. Participating in this journey together was building confidence. Companionship inspired us and elevated our experience from simply surviving to thriving.

The day before Thanksgiving was disconcertingly warm. The ice-rimmed shoreline had completely melted. Our campsite lost its snow cover, revealing grass, dirt, and duff. The chipmunk reemerged, darting about energetically as it added last-minute items to its larder. We were disappointed but not entirely surprised by this development: we have observed a general trend of warmer, shorter winters over the last two decades. Our dog-sled guiding season started a week later and ended a week earlier than it did fifteen years ago, and winters hardly ever dropped to 40 degrees below zero, as used to be common. According to Dr. Lee Frelich, a forest ecologist at the University of Minnesota, within a hundred years climate change will likely transform this pine and birch forest into an oak savannah.

Still, we decided to take advantage of the pleasant weather and celebrate Thanksgiving early, which allowed us to post photos on the actual holiday. A special dehydrated feast awaited: wild rice with cranberries and bison jerky, cornbread, potatoes, butternut squash, stuffing, smoked gouda cheese, smoked salmon, apple cider and rosehip tea to drink, and cinnamon apple slices for dessert formed a banquet atop our overturned canoe. Preparing all of our food in a timely fashion took some strategizing, given our limited supply of cooking pots and serving containers. We processed firewood, boiled water, and rehydrated dishes in every vessel we had. We ate and shot video and took photos. Then we ate some more and toasted with swigs of warm apple cider. Our food grew cold and we added layers of clothing as the sun dipped lower in the sky.

We were truly thankful for this feast that had been dehydrated, packed, and brought to us by friends. We were as isolated as we would be all year, and this was a reminder of everyone who loved and supported us.

SOON AFTER THANKSGIVING the temperatures began to drop. Colder nights caused a chill to seep into our sleeping bags if they weren't fully zipped and cinched. Skim ice in the bay extended four feet from shore. A thick mist rose off the lake like

Canoe turned Thanksgiving table

steam off a boiling pot. Out in the bay a couple lines on the water indicated something swimming in the fog. We assumed that our migratory avian neighbors had not all flown south. The moon rose over our icy bay. The main body of the lake was perfectly still. An astounding silence pervaded. No wind in the trees. No waves lapping on shore. No squirrels chattering or rustling in the carpet of fallen leaves. Just pure silence—broken only by our rhythmic breathing. In how many places in this country, we wondered, can you still experience true silence?

A sense of anxious anticipation gripped us as we surveyed our immediate surroundings for signs of the freeze-up. Shallower lakes nearby had completely frozen over. Despite all our previous wilderness travels, witnessing this process in one place provided a new education for us. All we could do was wait, chop holes in ice we found to measure its thickness, and check the temperature of Knife Lake's open water. Despite our measuring and hypothesizing about when we would be safely walking on the lakes, it was really anybody's guess. Nature has a way

Breaking ice on Knife Lake

of reminding us that we can never be completely in control, which can be aggravating for some but deeply instructive for those who are humble enough to pay attention.

One morning we emerged from the tent to find the soft light of a cloudless sunrise, a pinkish tint slowly growing behind the frosted trees to the east. The temperature had dropped to 5 degrees. The groaning and singing of the ever-expanding and thickening ice had signaled the shift during the night. A new swath of thin, clear ice spanned across the bay. On the other side of our peninsula the water steamed and the mostly full moon was still overhead. Frozen foam, ice bubbles, and frost crystals lined the shore. The loon pair was gone. What had been their cue to leave? Was it the air temperature? Water temperature? Had the fishing turned off? Their departure seemed to coincide with the otherworldly sounds of the previous night's ice growth.

The bald eagles were still around, though, patrolling the sky, silently perched on high pine branches, swooping down to catch an unsuspecting fish. In camp the red squirrels were our constant, chattering companions. Their pace of food stashing reached a frenzied crescendo. After placement of the prized source of winter sustenance—seeds or mushrooms—each squirrel would issue a loud chattering call, announcing the location of its stash to anyone who cared to know.

We reorganized our own food to see how long we could go before the next resupply and determined that we had enough food to last until December 19, a week later than planned. Still, what had first seemed like an extravagant amount of food would be carefully rationed from here on out. The thought of supplies was central as we weighed where and when to move. We would need to get closer to the edge of the Wilderness.

Sigurd Olson once wrote that "Wilderness offers [a] sense of cosmic purpose if we open our hearts and minds to its possibilities." The extended freeze-up was stressful, but it forced us to slow down and immerse ourselves in the sliver of the vast wilderness that surrounded us. We had spent thousands of days in wilderness around the world,

Knife Lake's icy shoreline

but never before had we been without timelines or schedules, nor any agenda other than to bear witness to it. We passed hours watching the clouds float across the sky and listening to the ice sing, the wolves howl, and the wind sweep over the ridges.

On December 1, we paddled the length of Knife Lake. In the narrows south of Robbins Island the canoe plowed through undulating pancakes of ice until running into a solid sheet. With no path forward we backtracked and headed to the north side of the island, where a thin band of open water allowed our passage. At that point we decided to set out for the smaller, completely frozen Vera Lake. At the end of the portage we surveyed the ice and found that it was not yet thick enough to cross. A slushy layer was developing from the snowflakes currently falling on the ice. Unsure of the best course of action, we set up our tent on a flat snow-covered rock. Inside the tent drips drummed against the nylon as melted snow fell from tree branches. An occasional loud plop startled us as a big glob of snow dropped.

The next day we anxiously trekked down to the lake at first light and were

relieved to see that it was covered in a gray layer of sloppy slush. Several inches of snow would have insulated the ice, but the slush would freeze as nighttime temperatures dropped. With time on our hands, we decided to explore, donning our dry suits and life jackets. We followed wolf tracks skirting the shoreline. Otters had left evidence of their passing, too, via slide marks and paw prints frozen into the surface of the ice. There was something reassuring about this record of other animals that had ventured out onto the lake.

After dark, we were in the tent working on dinner when we heard wolves howling nearby. This wasn't the distant call of a pack wandering miles away. Instead it reminded us of the numerous times we've camped with sled dogs bedded down just outside our tent. We could even hear one or two of the wolves making a kind of sharp short bark. And then, just as suddenly as their howl had begun, it ended. A faint rustling of snow-coated leaves was all we heard of their stealthy maneuvering past our tent.

We imagined this pack of wolves cruising along the portage trail, climbing up from Knife Lake in the

Waiting for Vera Lake to freeze solid

moonlight and sniffing our tracks. As they neared our tent—this glowing, alien object—they cut into the cover of the scraggly oak trees. They would have smelled us: our sweat, the wool and synthetic clothing we were wearing, the woodsmoke, the rice and lentils we were cooking for dinner. Had they howled in greeting or warning? Perhaps, slightly perplexed by our presence, they moved on toward Vera Lake and we were soon forgotten as their nightly wandering ensued.

THOUGH WE HAD tested the ice the previous day, we woke up before dawn and walked down to the lake. The sky had been clear all night and the temperature had dropped significantly. A hole chopped in the newer ice revealed three inches. This was our opportunity to move. We packed up as quickly as we could and ate a hurried breakfast.

Despite the rushed packing, we looked for tracks. The wolves had come right up the trail and then veered into the woods a few yards from our tent. Eventually they made their way down to Vera Lake and out onto the ice, heading in the same direction we would go.

We gathered ropes to haul our canoe, and to use as throw ropes in case one of us broke through. The sun rose as we loaded the last of our gear in our canoe. We were keen to get going before the day warmed with the sunlight. We slipped Yaktrax on the bottoms of our boots for traction. We were dressed in warm layers, dry suits, and life jackets. Ice picks hung from our necks. The axe was easily accessible in the canoe, for checking ice. We had even packed an emergency clothing bag with a down jacket, puffy pants, and wool socks. We both knew this was the riskiest ice we had ever traveled on and we almost expected immersion. We just hoped we wouldn't both fall through at the same time.

Preparing to travel across Vera Lake

WINTER

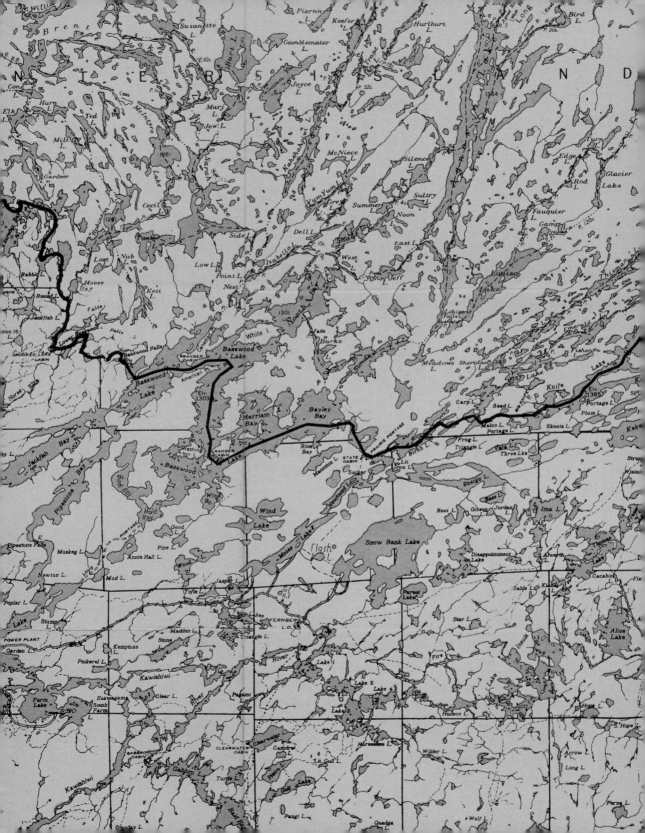

We were nervous as we cut away from land, crossing a little bay to the shaded south shore. One of us hauled the canoe with a ten-foot rope while the other walked ahead to check the ice conditions. The newly frozen lake crackled under our feet as we gingerly picked our way across, keeping at least twenty feet apart at all times. Relief washed over us when we reached the other side and saw a ribbon of slightly thicker ice stretching ahead.

We skirted the land, leery of any variation in the shoreline. Whenever we came to a change in the color of the ice, we cut a hole with the axe to check it. When we opted to cross one more bay, moving as fast as we could, again the ice crackled. We relaxed slightly once we realized the noise was made by a thin layer of bad ice on top of a solid clear base. Along the far shore we followed the fresh tracks of the wolves we had heard the night before.

By the time we finished the portage to Ensign Lake the temperature had risen to 45 degrees. The ice there was thicker, but with the warmth and sunlight it would quickly degrade. Halfway down the lake we paused for lunch, sitting down on the ice and relishing the cool that radiated from its damp surface. We laughed about how absurd it felt to be lounging in the sun next to our canoe on the ice as we ate. These six hours were some of the tensest—and riskiest—we had

Hauling firewood back to camp

ever experienced. In our seven-mile walk, we had drawn on years of dogsledding, ice-reading, and cold-water paddling skills. In many ways the new experiences and challenges we face are what draw us back to wild places. Wilderness pushes us and makes us better, leaving us more confident in ourselves and our ability to work together.

On an island campsite we fell back into our usual routine, as warm weather made travel impossible. We stocked up on firewood the next morning, while the ice was still safe to walk on, and spent the following days processing the wood, cooking, writing, and listening to the radio. We chopped a hole in the ice with the axe to gather drinking and cooking water from the lake—something we would do at each new campsite throughout the winter. Occasionally we heard wolves howling, and one day a small plane circled nearby— most likely biologists tracking the pack. In the not-so-distant past, northern Minnesota was the only place in the continental United States where gray wolves hadn't been totally eradicated. Though wolf populations have come back in other

pockets of wilderness throughout the US, thanks to their addition to the Endangered Species List in 1974, the Boundary Waters and the surrounding forest are still home to the largest concentration of wolves in the lower forty-eight states.

The ice deteriorated to the point where we couldn't leave our island for a few days. It made us sad to watch the ice melt in the middle of December, as if it was spring. What once held our weight and the loaded canoe broke apart and opened up during a sunny afternoon. Our food was almost gone by the time cold weather made the ice safe again. Traveling light and fast, we took off on a reconnaissance mission to survey the route to Moose Lake, where much-needed supplies would be brought in. We followed the winter portages, which snake through bogs to avoid water kept open by current. Bogs are often slow to freeze—the decomposition of plants produces heat—and a couple times our feet punched through the ice into a few inches of water. Fortunately, rubber boots kept our feet warm and dry.

The land and ice told the story of the wolves that had recently passed

Amy tests her drysuit

through. Old tracks were embedded in the ice, following a similar shore-skirting route as us. Fresh scat and occasional scratches indicated that wolves had traveled this way after the ice firmed up and they no longer left obvious tracks. Depressions in the tall grass along shore told us wolves bedded down there for the night.

We made it as far as Horseshoe Island, on Newfound Lake, before we were stopped by open water. The sky was pale gray and so was the ice; the deeper water beyond was a dark gash. A haze of fog rose up from its surface, obscuring the distant shore. Moose Lake would probably be open, too. At least we knew we could move significantly closer to the resupply point.

THE LACK OF sun began to wear on us. We rationed our battery use, limiting posts and only listening to the radio for twenty minutes each day. We spent a lot of time reading, but had to constrict our

Navigating open water into Splash Lake

Kindle time, reading one chapter of Elizabeth Kolbert's *The Sixth Extinction* a day aloud. We relished our one physical book, *Indian Creek Chronicles* by Pete Fromm. At least the coffee would hold out; we frequently made two or three batches a day. Circumnavigating our little island on foot kept us sane.

After breakfast one morning Dave walked down the latrine trail wondering how many more times over the next few months he'd end up dusting the snow off the latrine before his morning constitutional. As he sat there watching the flakes gently fall, a snowshoe hare raced by, a blur of white and brown. Right on its tail was a pine marten, eyes fixed on its quarry. In the heat of the chase, did they even realize that they ran right past his feet?

We would gladly trade running water for a few interesting moments like that over the next ten and a half months. How often do you get to watch a predator chase its prey in your bathroom? That rabbit had been hopping around our campsite for several days, rustling the leaf litter and even bumping its way along the edge of the tent as it wandered through the willows. We couldn't help but wonder who won the chase, secretly hoping that the hare outran its pursuer. But Dave couldn't get the terror in the hare's eyes, or the intense primal focus of the pine marten, out of his mind.

On December 16, we were keen to get going early. Snow was in the forecast and there was talk of an attempt to reach us with the much-needed resupply. Massive wet flakes began to fall, accumulating on packs and clothing as we packed the canoe. We decided to paddle through the narrows to Splash Lake rather than walk the winter portage, and by the time we reached open water an inch of snow had fallen. Looking back, we couldn't make out our campsite or the island we had come from. All we could see was a mass of white.

We walked tentatively on the slushy ice and clambered over rocks along shore to slide the canoe across rotten ice and into open water before climbing in. A beaver swam ahead of us, its nose sticking out of the water. A raven flew above. Snowflakes melted upon contact with the dark water. As we reached the end of the open water, we eyed a patch of ice that was close to a rocky protuberance. We rammed it and the bow rode up on top of the ice. This maneuver was so bizarre that we realized we needed to share the moment. So we pushed back off the ice, turned on our GoPro, and rammed up onto the ice again.

That brief paddle was the easiest part of our day. After dragging the canoe onto the ice, we realized that slush and snow were instantly freezing to its bottom. We quickly unloaded and flipped the canoe. Our paddles became scrapers as we frantically tried to remove the slush before it solidified on the hull.

Whiteout conditions obscured our vision. Hidden pockets of slush and four inches of new snow greeted us on Newfound Lake. It was harder and harder to pull the canoe as the drifts accumulated. Once we reached the south side of Horseshoe Island, we walked to the ice edge to get a good look down the length of the lake. It was wide open as far as we could see. Hauling the canoe had kept us warm, but when we stopped, we grew cold. We paced and did jumping jacks until we saw a small motorboat approaching.

We had three visitors. Willy Vosburgh, resort owner and expert towboat driver, nosed the boat onto the ice and tentatively climbed out of the bow to pull it onto safe ice. He was followed by Steve Piragis and Donna, Willy's English bulldog. She was a ball of muscle and energy, running around in a doggy life jacket.

Their trip had been no small feat. Steve and Willy had rammed the motorboat through pans of ice and then carefully hauled it over short sections that were too thick to break through. Unfortunately, when we peeked inside the portage packs we noticed that there were no food supplies— just warmer sleeping bags and some fresh fruit and vegetables that Steve had brought as a surprise. Off they went, back to the Moose Lake landing. Waiting again, we each ate a crisp apple from the stash. They were

bursting with juice and flavor. Being deprived of fresh fruit for weeks amplified our sensory experience; those were the best apples of our lives.

More comforting than the food headed our way was the knowledge that weeks of solitude had come to an end. We had remained in frequent communication with the Campaign to Save the Boundary Waters staff, to be sure. Most days we spent at least a couple hours sharing photos, blogging, posting on social media, journaling, and doing interviews via email. We were part of a well-organized team working to protect this place, but Steve and Willy were the first humans we had seen in a month. By the time we would run low on our new rations, all sorts of people would be traveling into the Boundary Waters by ski, snowshoe, and dogsled to visit us.

After the return of our guests, and their second departure, we cooked dinner, savoring every word they had said, the expressions on their faces, and the absurd image of Donna scampering around on the ice in her life jacket. Clearly, our visitors were leaving indelible memories that remain woven into our year in the wilderness.

The view from our campsite one morning revealed churning, steaming

Exploring the ice edge on Newfound Lake

water, riled up by a strong wind from the west. We decided to walk as close to the edge of the ice as we dared to check it out. We had been walking all over that area for several days, so we didn't bother to put on our dry suits. Fifty feet from the edge, we checked the ice with the axe. Water came burbling up disconcertingly soon after just a couple of whacks. It was only about one and a half inches thick, well below the Department of Natural Resources' recommended four inches, so we carefully backtracked and moved toward the center of the bay.

We were slightly concerned by the state of the ice, but felt comfortable in the spot we had retreated to. Dave set up the tripod for a photo of the sea smoke, and as he did, the ice below him sagged ever so slightly. A handful of moments in our lives cause us to cringe whenever we remember them; moments where, in hindsight, the warning signs were glaringly obvious and our survival can only be attributed to dumb luck. This was one of those moments. The waves we'd been watching had worn away the ice from below.

Dave noticed the sag. In one fluid motion he dove and threw the camera sideways. A wave radiated out from the spot where he had just been standing, followed by a sickening cracking sound and a splash. Dave's lunge had saved him from complete immersion. For a split second his lower body was in the water, but his torso remained on the surface of miraculously unbroken ice. Shouting "Get the camera, get the camera!" he quickly slithered toward our footprints, knowing the safest spot was ice that had previously held our weight. By the time Dave got back to camp, his pants were encrusted in ice. We hung the wet clothes up to dry and sat by the wood stove, eating warm quesadillas. This little drama had the potential to yield a great social media post—but then we realized that our parents would probably freak out, and it was just the beginning of the winter. So we agreed: the incident wouldn't be divulged until we exited the Boundary Waters.

AS CHRISTMAS APPROACHED, we strung up solar-powered lights on our tent. Initially this was less for our benefit and more for an interview with the *Minneapolis Star Tribune*. But at some point we realized it was the first time we had hung up Christmas lights together. And although we were attaching the lights to a tent in the Boundary Waters, our process would have looked familiar to many: debate about the design, untangling, struggling, exchanging some terse words—and lights that wouldn't turn on when plugged into the solar battery. After sunset, we realized that these lights had a sensor and only glowed when it was dark out. In the end we came to enjoy the lights, which added cheer to the longest nights of the year.

We were stymied by increasingly limited power. Short days and cloudy weather had made our solar panels ineffective for several weeks. We had plenty of downtime as we waited for the lakes to freeze, but we

Ice conditions were always changing

were unable to charge our cameras and communication equipment. If we're stuck hanging around camp, we thought, at least we could be organizing our finances, writing articles, or reading about Ernest Shackleton's 1914–1917 Antarctic expedition. Even our Kindle was almost out of power.

On Christmas Eve the sound of the tent flapping in the wind woke us before first light. Unable to sleep, we built a fire in the woodstove and shared holiday memories. As a kid, Dave had alternated spending Christmas with his mother and father. Amy's grandmother used to spend weeks baking traditional Norwegian Christmas cookies. This would be the first Christmas without her—not because we were in the wilderness, but because she had passed away the previous summer.

Our isolation was taking its toll, and melancholy threatened to establish a tone for the day. So we experimented with baking our own Norwegian Christmas cookies, sandbakelse, under the woodstove. We still didn't have a bridge between us and the outside world, but at least we could keep a few holiday traditions alive. We mixed up the buttery almond-flavored dough and pressed tablespoons of it into a dozen little tins. Most of the first batch stuck to the metal because the bottoms were undercooked. On the next round we rotated the tins from over and under the stove—and the cookies were no different than if they had been baked in an ordinary oven.

Calling our families later that day cheered us both up. We went for a walk to Moose Lake, wearing our dry suits and cautiously checking the ice. It felt momentous to finally walk through the narrows and onto the main body of Newfound. Periodically we hacked a hole in the ice with the axe, each time revealing a solid four inches of ice. Even Moose was safe to walk on. Frozen lakes were the best Christmas gift ever. Soon we would be free to roam them at will.

WE TRADED OUR canoe for toboggans on December 28, another snowy day. That morning we loaded

Sandbakelse baked in the Wilderness

the canoe with items to jettison—paddles, life jackets, and other unnecessary equipment—and walked toward the Wilderness boundary. We had never expected to keep our canoe this long; climate change had certainly affected our plans.

As we walked, the Northern Tier Boy Scout base came into view. This was the first time we had seen any buildings since entering the Boundary Waters. The forested hillside nearby was dotted with cabins. The geometric shapes of their rooftops looked out of place to our eyes, which had become accustomed to rounded edges and irregular patterns. Strands of smoke curled upward, signaling warm interiors.

We checked in with each other. How did we feel seeing these bastions of comfort and signifiers of the civilized world? We had expected to feel desire. We had worried that we would want to leave the Wilderness for a cozy house. We looked at those cabins for a good long while, imagining their interiors, but no sense of longing welled up in our guts. We both felt indifferent to those buildings. We had everything we needed out here; this was where we belonged.

After making the trade, we returned to our campsite, strapped on our newly acquired skis, and cruised down the untracked lake. A couple inches of powder on solid ice provided excellent glide. We were giddy to move so much faster than walking—until we stumbled upon a massive slush pocket. Like a landmine, it had been an invisible puddle, concealed by snow. We plodded out and scraped off our skis.

Our time alone was over—and so were our first hundred days in the Boundary Waters. Over the next week our social calendar would bring more visitors. We hadn't seen Jason since whitefish netting, so he and his friend, Sarah, arrived on New Year's Eve, establishing a sense of festivity at our campsite. We played soccer with a beach ball on the ice, each of our breaths a white cloud trailing behind us in the dim light—until the ball popped in the cold. As the temperature dropped and darkness descended, Jason and Sarah dispensed glittery hats and goofy glasses. We posed for photos well before midnight, because we figured it was unlikely we would be awake to officially ring in the New Year.

As the stove warmed the frosted walls of the tent, we set a large pot on top and concocted glögg. We

Waiting patiently while we gather firewood

were a little apprehensive when it came time to ignite the glögg, but no harm was done to the tent. We watched a blue flame dance on the dark liquid, like the northern lights contained in a kettle. And we did manage to stay up until midnight after all, chattering and laughing and feasting.

In the early afternoon on January 2 we heard barking dogs on the lake and went to take a look. Frank Moe, our friend from Sled Dogs to Saint Paul, cruised along behind an eight-dog team, towing our expedition manager, Levi, on skis. They arrived in a frenzy of barking and our quiet little campsite was suddenly filled with exuberance.

After Frank jammed in two snow hooks behind the sled to keep his team from running off without him, we gave him a hug and set to work. One hundred and fifty pounds of dog food and other supplies were unloaded from his sled and replaced with items we were trading in. We used ice

Traveling by toboggan at last

screws to set up our little three-dog stake-out line, a cable with a couple feet of chain attached in three separate spots. We transferred the three dogs we were borrowing for the winter—Acorn, Tina, and Tank—to the line. Acorn was Tina and Tank's mother—and Frank's favorite lead dog. At twelve years old, she was slowing down but showing no desire to retire. At

nine years old, Tina and Tank were a bit more boisterous in their desire to hit the trail and run at a fast pace. Acorn and Tina were petite in comparison to Tank, who weighed twice as much.

When it was time for Frank to go, he somberly knelt down by each dog he was leaving to say good-bye. We helped turn his team around, Levi grabbed the towrope, and they sped

away as our three new dogs barked like crazy. Within just twenty minutes our team had more than doubled in size. We decided there was no time like the present for our first skijor with the dogs, and clipped into our skis while attempting to hold them back.

Away we flew across Newfound and Moose Lakes, following Frank's fresh tracks. Acorn and Tina pulled Dave while Tank pulled Amy. As we neared the Wilderness boundary, we were unsure if the dogs would heed the commands of two strangers asking them to deviate from their owner's tracks. Speeding along at seven miles per hour, we told the girls to turn right. At "Tina, Acorn, gee . . . gee" they began veering right. Another "gee . . . gee" and they had spun

180 degrees into untracked snow. The dogs raced back toward camp without so much as a glance over their shoulders or change in speed.

Over the course of the winter we would come to intimately know and depend on these dogs. We often wondered what they thought of all this. Were any of them homesick? If so, they did not let on. Did they believe they were on a grand adventure? Only Tank had some previous experience traveling in the Boundary Waters. Too slow to make the cut for the race team, Tank had previously been loaned out to the Voyageur Outward Bound School and Camp Menogyn. Tina and Acorn were racing dogs through and through; camping and pulling heavy toboggans was new to them. Having worked with many other sled dogs, however, we knew there are three things they love: food, pulling, and attention from humans. We were confident we could give them plenty of these.

WITH THE LAKES finally frozen and our means of winter travel delivered, we felt like kids who had been deprived of recess for a month. It would take us a couple weeks to grow accustomed to the added dog chores and packing toboggans instead of a canoe. During our first morning with the dogs we slowly packed the toboggans, weighing the optimal place for each pack and piece of gear, placing heavy items low and near the center to decrease the likelihood of tipping over. We tied the toboggans together, one in front of the other, and hooked all three dogs to the front. Acorn and Tina were in lead, with Tank providing most of the power in wheel, the rear position on a dog team. We would take turns hooked into the back of the train with a skijoring harness. On the command of "OK, let's go," the dogs flew across the flat lake, seemingly unencumbered by the four hundred pounds dragging behind them.

Once we got to the steep incline of our first portage, however, the dogs stalled, unaccustomed to so much resistance. The weight of the toboggans must have felt just like Frank

Amy skijoring with Tina and Acorn

applying the brakes. Confused by our words of encouragement, Acorn and Tina turned to look at us on every steep hill—and that first portage had a lot of hills. We found over time that it worked well for one of us to assume the position of a fourth dog to help pull the larger toboggan over a portage while the other hauled the lighter one separately. Within a few days Tina, Tank, and Acorn learned that the added resistance didn't mean to stop and they pulled hard even when our pace slowed to a crawl. Soon all it took was a snap of the gangline or a tug of the toboggan and away they would go, with us scrambling to follow.

We fell into a rhythm of base camping for a few days or a week at a time, heading out on skijoring day trips to explore our surroundings. Setting up, breaking down, and moving camp in the winter is a lot of work, requiring an hour to pack in the morning and almost two hours to set up at the end of the day. And since sharing our story was at the very heart of this mission, solar panels, batteries, and communication gear made our load particularly heavy. If we were exhausted

Soaking up the sun

AMY AND DAVE FREEMAN · 117

in the evening we would struggle to achieve our mission. Like many animals of the boreal forest, we would need to conserve energy to survive the winter. The short days and deep cold of midwinter caused our pace to slow even more and brought the value of shelter, warmth, and food into sharp focus.

Skijoring quickly became the favorite mode of transportation for us and the dogs. Without the toboggans, the dogs got to run at a pace they were used to, and we loved the speed and freedom of gliding over a frozen expanse. We were five creatures venturing across an untracked sea of white, content to stay out until dusk, because our tent, woodpile, and stash of food would be waiting back at camp. After completing a run, we unharnessed the dogs, put on their jackets, and set up their beds. Often mushers cut spruce boughs for their dogs to sleep on, but this violates the leave-no-trace principles of wilderness travel. Instead we provided a foam sleeping pad for each dog. With a blanket added, the dogs were well insulated from the snow and ice.

Our small group slowly worked its way to Wood Lake, where we would be meeting friends from Grand Marais: Andy Keith, John Oberholtzer (O.B.), and O.B.'s kids—Hazel and Cy. We picked out one of the few non-slushy spots in a bay to set up camp on the ice. Slush is often referred to as the bane of the Boundary Waters—and this winter was shaping up to be one of the worst in recent memory. All we could do was hope below-zero weather would arrive soon and freeze the mess we had just slogged through.

We skijored to the portage and were overjoyed to see our friends emerge from the woods. Each hauled a small but overloaded plastic sled. We made a substantial train out of all four and the dogs helped pull their gear to our campsite. Before long we were all sitting in O.B.'s mint-green tent, absorbing the warmth produced by his massive woodstove.

O.B. had accompanied Dave for a portion of the Border Route Expedition of 2001, when Dave skied the Minnesota–Ontario border through the Boundary Waters with a sled dog named Tundra. That expedition had sparked the idea for the Wilderness Classroom. As Dave was preparing to head out on the mostly solo venture, his mother insisted he get a satellite phone so he could call for help if he fell through the ice. Despite his efforts to convince her

Hazel loved feeding the dogs

that making a phone call would be a low priority if he did fall through the ice, she persisted. Right around this time, the technology to connect to the Internet and post postage-stamp sized pictures became available. So before blogging was even a widely used term, Dave had created a basic website and convinced five teachers to follow the journey with their classes.

Andy was no stranger to wilderness expeditions himself, having written *Afloat Again, Adrift* about paddling the three paths water takes from Minnesota: down the Mississippi River to New Orleans, north to Hudson Bay, and through the Great Lakes to the Saint Lawrence Seaway.

Our friends' last night on Wood Lake was the coldest of the winter so far: 24 degrees below zero. We woke up in the morning to Andy's footsteps outside our tent, followed by a plea to take some wood from our pile. Out of concern for the kids' comfort they had kept their fire burning all night, and now they were out of fuel.

We bade them farewell after breakfast and, a few hours later, greeted a contingent of guides from Wintergreen Dogsled Lodge. While skijoring with these coworkers and long-time friends to our campsite, the differences between our dogs became apparent. The Wintergreen dogs were Canadian Inuits, while Acorn, Tina, and Tank were Alaskan huskies. Inuit dogs are like four-wheel drive trucks: they're hearty and can pull a lot of weight. Alaskan huskies, on the other hand, are like race cars: they require more care because of their thinner coats, but they sure can fly. Back at camp, we put jackets on Acorn, Tina and Tank while the Inuit dogs contentedly curled up to nap in the snow, their thick fur making them impervious to the cold. All the humans settled around the woodstove and the tent was soon filled with jovial new voices.

THE CHILL GAVE way to temperatures in the teens and we moved camp again. Though we wanted the deep cold to keep slush away, life was generally easier when the temperature was above zero. Taking a hand out of a mitten to tie a knot didn't have to be done with frantic haste. The dogs didn't need booties on their feet for every run; instead, we just rubbed salve on their paws. But perhaps the best aspect of warmer temperatures was the improved glide of skis and toboggans. Below zero, snow can feel like sandpaper under one's skis regardless of the wax applied. When the snow is somewhat warmer, the friction with the skis and toboggans melts the snow ever so slightly and they work as they should, sliding over a thin layer of water for a split second. We had also experienced just enough deep cold to crust over the slush pockets, but not freeze them all the way through. On warmer days slush was less bothersome because it did not freeze to skis and toboggans.

On Basswood Lake, we headed across Hoist Bay and then onto the Four Mile Portage. The Four Mile is relatively flat, an old railroad grade that was once used to haul logs and is now a musher's highway of sorts, connecting Fall Lake with Basswood. From our campsite on Fall we watched the passing dog teams. Several ice fishermen set up shelters nearby, and we entertained a parade

The dogs were always ready to run

AMY AND DAVE FREEMAN · 121

of visitors who came out to deliver supplies and chat. The Boundary Waters sees more visitors than any other wilderness in the country. While most of that use occurs in the summertime, it was exciting to see how many people were venturing out in the winter too: sleeping under the stars, skiing, snowshoeing, dog-sledding, ice fishing, or just enjoying a walk on a frozen lake.

A few days later, our little team painted a meandering line on the white canvas of Jackfish Bay. A river otter crossed the bay directly in front of us, moving fast. We could identify it from a long way off because no other animal moves quite like an otter in the winter. The dark slender figure took a few bounding steps and then slid on its belly. Step, step, slide, step, step, slide—quite an efficient mode of locomotion. When the otter turned around and started running back the way it had come from, the dogs noticed. Their speed picked up and Dave was dragged along. Eventually the otter turned again, running and sliding in the direction we were heading. So the dogs gave chase, and slowly gained on the otter. Not wanting to distress the animal, Dave began

snowplowing as hard as he could, eventually stopping the team.

It was then that we spotted five dark shapes off the point of an island. We tipped over the back toboggan to keep the dogs in place while we got the camera and the otter disappeared. Our first thought had been that the shapes were wolves. But as we stood there and the shapes remained perfectly still, we began to doubt ourselves. Were they just rocks, or driftwood? We took several photos and moved on.

As we passed the island, we glanced over our shoulders. The dark shapes had rounded the point. They were indeed wolves, and they were following us. When we stopped, so did they. When we started moving again, they tracked behind. We continued moving, but suppressed an instinct to speed up. While these animals very well could chase us down and attack us, we knew they wouldn't. Still, for a moment we identified with species of prey like snowshoe hares or white-tail deer rather than the predators we generally are.

We set up camp on Tin Can Mike Lake, with several recent modifications. We staked the tent with ice screws in only four places. Each day we became a bit more efficient at setting up and breaking down camp. Experiments in pitching our tent differently led to adopting a new method. We shifted from anchoring our tent with skis or sticks buried in the snow to sticks stuck in holes drilled by ice screws. Despite the thousands of nights we had spent winter camping, there was always something new to learn. Constant problem-solving is one of the intangible values that comes with time spent in the wilderness. There is always something new to learn, some system that can be made more efficient. Every day is filled with challenges that must be overcome.

We also changed our approach to traveling. Instead of setting out across an untracked lake with our loaded toboggans, we took to breaking a trail the day before we intended to move camp. It meant traveling the same trail two or three times, but it greatly decreased the amount of effort expended by the dogs and by us. Our snowshoes packed a track that would firm up overnight and we could remove any obstacles on the portages. Any slush pockets we exposed would also freeze solid. From Tin Can Mike Lake, we hunted for and broke open

the seldom-used winter portage that follows an old railroad grade. We were occasionally slowed by alders and willows. We brought the dogs, though we each had an occasional fall when they kept pulling while our snowshoes were mired in branches or hummocks. If we didn't get up right away, Tank got in the habit of walking back to check on us, whining and licking our faces. Any anger or frustration instantly melted away with this display of unwavering affection. Eventually we made our way past a rusting car in the woods—one of several remnants of an old logging camp near the shore of Fourtown Lake.

Back at camp we basked in the sun. All our chores—processing wood, gathering water, soaking dog food—seemed easy in the warmth and increased daylight. The moon rose in the east, full and enormous. The darkening sky left a few wispy pink clouds behind for a while.

The next day we packed up and headed down the trail we had broken. For the most part, the going was smooth. Ski tracks on Fourtown Lake would be the last signs of humans we would see for a week; all other tracks we crossed were made by the animal inhabitants of this wilderness.

WE TUCKED INTO the jack pines and balsam fir along the north shore of Gun Lake. That night we struggled to fall asleep—our bodies on high alert in new surroundings. Snowshoe hare tracks had been abundant here, so we attributed any stirring in the alders to them. But a new sound caused us to sit upright and puzzle about its source. It was a single note, repeated: "toot, toot, toot, toot, toot, toot." We figured it was an owl, but its call was different than that of the one owl we could confidently identify by sound—a barred owl with its familiar "who cooks for you" call. Days later, a friend who was familiar with owls of the northwoods helped us identify it as a male northern saw-whet owl, practicing his mating call.

The next day, though the tent sagged from an inch of new snow and the dogs' beds were covered, the air temperature was surprisingly warm—28 degrees. Dave stripped off all his clothes and spent several hours typing a blog post, with the tent door wide open. We each had plenty of writing to do in the evenings, trading off the weekly podcast and blog posts for the Campaign to Save the Boundary Waters, while also producing online articles for *National Geographic Adventure* and *Canoe & Kayak*, educational Wilderness Classroom updates, and our own daily social media. Despite all this rapidly published reporting, Amy often stayed up late recording more personal thoughts and observations in her journal.

We awoke to a veneer of ice on the tent and rain falling from the sky in late January. Our mukluks punched through an icy crust on top of the snow. We dashed our plans for an ambitious day trip in favor of remaining warm and dry in our tent. We saw this as another lesson slowly learned from the Wilderness—and a luxury of spending a year there. There is no point in fighting the elements, suffering unnecessarily, or taking dangerous risks. We've learned that it is better to wait for favorable weather, and work with nature.

When we finally did head toward

Frost slowly melts off our axe handle

Slush-covered boots were common

Angleworm Lake, an intermittent snow was falling and a light wind was blowing from the northwest. The portage from Gull to Home Lake is 277 rods and we were apparently the first winter travelers to trek across it. Snow-laden alders drooped over much of the trail and we slowly worked our way through. After several hours of skijoring and clearing branches, we were rewarded by the sight of a narrow untracked lake. Surrounded by significant topography, we felt as if we were in a canyon skijoring down the middle. Snow-frosted granite cliffs and boulders surrounded us. We skied to the south end of the lake, ate lunch, and turned around. We felt a sense of profound satisfaction from the hard physical labor of breaking that trail open with no more purpose than to see the lake at its end.

A WEEK OF solitude was broken by contact with a Wintergreen group that had followed our tracks to Gun Lake. Sitting around their campfire, we learned that their trip had been fraught with slush despite our trail breaking the previous week. The temperature dropped well below zero during the night and we fell asleep confident that we would easily glide along the trail that had just been reopened by the dogsledders.

The next morning, a south wind was oddly warm in contrast to the weather of the previous night. Snow began falling and accumulating on every piece of equipment before it was hurriedly tucked into a toboggan. Just halfway across Gun we hit slush. We diverted, only to encounter more slush. The Wintergreen crew was heading the same way and they passed us as we scraped our skis and toboggans. We followed in their tracks, with Acorn, Tank, and Tina freshly motivated by the scent of over a dozen sled dogs on the trail ahead of them.

Still, slush ruled the day. We would make forward progress until the toboggans bogged down with so much frozen slush that the dogs stopped. That was our cue to pull scrapers out of our pockets and set to work. The trail packed by the dogsledders was wider than our toboggans, which actually resulted in them tracking poorly and occasionally tipping over. Exhausted, we flipped on our headlamps as we emerged onto Tin Can Mike and focused their beams on the Wintergreen tracks. Dots of light from other campers were visible in the distance. We tucked in next to a cliff face and proceeded to set up camp in the dark, our world reduced to the patch of ice illuminated by our headlamps.

We had a frustrating day and there would be more to follow, but we came to accept these trying moments. What else could we do? We were in the midst of an exceptionally slushy winter with erratic weather. El Niño, climate change, and the nature of the Boundary Waters lakes had conspired to make our travels difficult. Between the conditions and scheduled visits near entry points, we didn't journey as far as we had originally intended. We spent weeks bouncing back and forth between Tin Can Mike, Gun, and Angleworm. It

WINTER

began to feel as if the culmination of our activity this winter would be to break open the same familiar trails over and over again as a dump of snow or strong wind obliterated them shortly after their creation. White ribbons comprised of dog footprints and ski tracks that quickly disappeared under fresh snow were like layers of sediment in a river bottom forming an esker. In the spring, when the snow melted, these ribbons would reappear on the surface of the dark ice.

And so Mother Nature succeeded in teaching us a lesson in humility. Our travels in wild places have never been motivated by the desire to conquer nature. History is full of examples of explorers being too set in their ways to adapt and then paying the ultimate price by freezing to death or starving. If one wants to survive out here, one must be observant and adapt. Going with the flow is the only way one can survive—and even thrive—in a wild place.

SEVERAL DAYS LATER, as the toboggan train came to a halt on our way back to Gun, Tank licked the tip of Acorn's tail. Intrigued by this new behavior, we took a closer look at Acorn's tail and saw a raw red spot where there should have been fur. As we set up camp on Gun, possible causes of the injury raced through our minds. Had Tina bitten her mom's tail? Was it a cancerous growth? Maybe it had frozen to the stake-out line? We cleaned the wound, bandaged it, and called Frank. He diagnosed frostbite and emphasized that we couldn't let the wound refreeze. Poor Acorn! Another stretch of below-zero weather was in the forecast, so we gained a new tentmate. She seemed to know that her stay in the tent was contingent upon not urinating on our sleeping bags or knocking over the woodstove. She remained curled up on her pad, basking in the warmth of the stove while we ate dinner. That night, like new parents, we woke whenever she stirred. But each time she just shook, spun in a circle, and settled back down to sleep. Acorn didn't spend another night on the stake-out line for the rest of the winter.

A couple days later, as we were preparing to move camp from Gun to Angleworm, a gray flash across the white surface of the lake caught our attention. A wolf was trotting across the bay in front of us, toward the portage to Gull Lake. We grabbed the camera and Acorn, in case she had any urge to greet this new arrival. Standing out on the ice in our long underwear, we observed a pack of five wolves, lounging just down the shore from us. Three were lying down in the sun with their legs stretched out on the ice while the other two sat upright. Surely they were aware of our presence, but their body language suggested that they were completely unbothered by it. Eventually they wandered across the portage, leaving behind scent markings that greatly intrigued Acorn, Tina, and Tank when we traveled the same way an hour later.

That night, as we set up camp on Angleworm, we heard voices echoing off the rock walls surrounding the steep-sided lake and figured that some folks were passing on the trail that circled the lake. When the noise continued well into the evening, we realized that there was a group camping nearby—our first neighbors since October.

We spent a warm overcast day traveling to North and South Hegman Lakes. We headed into the bog at the south end of Angleworm and then got on a seldom-used mile and a half–long trail with multiple ups and downs and tangles. Tina adamantly insisted on turning around, as she pulled in the direction we had just come from, dragging Acorn with her. The trail was too narrow to have Acorn and Tina side by side anyway, so we set Acorn loose. She took the lead, happily trekking down the trail, occasionally pausing to smell a vole tunnel or snowshoe hare track in the snow. Tank and Tina were keen to follow their mom, solving the problem. Opening up that trail was arduous, though. We trudged through deep snow, diverted around deadfall, and occasionally lost the trail entirely. Tease Lake was one big soupy puddle of slush hidden under several inches of snow. The good news was that the temperature was so warm the slush didn't stick to skis or dog paws. It took us most of the day just to reach North Hegman.

We stopped to pay our respects at a pictograph site on the north end of the lake, perhaps the most visited in the Boundary Waters. We had come to this spot many times before, but each time we were newly intrigued by the origin of these ochre images on the rock. A human figure stands with arms outstretched. Three canoes drift above. A male moose runs below, followed by a smaller creature with pointy ears, short legs, and a long tail. According to Carl Gawboy—an author, artist, professor, and member of the Bois Forte Band of Chippewa—the pictographs represent constellations. The human figure is the Wintermaker to the Anishinaabe—or, Orion— which, in the winter, at this location, is standing upright in the night sky to the southwest. The figures in the canoes are paddling through what the Anishinaabe call the Path of Souls, or the Milky Way. The moose coincides with the Great Square of Pegasus for its body and Lacerta for its antlers. If one looks closely at the moose, it is apparent that paint was omitted in two small dots indicating where its heart belongs—and coinciding with a star located within the Great Square of Pegasus. All these figures can be seen together in the early evenings of mid-March.

Leaving an offering of tobacco would have been the respectful thing to do, but we had none. So we broke off a piece of a Clif Bar and wedged it in a crack below the ancient drawings. We wondered about their creator, standing in a canoe, dabbing the paint of iron hematite and boiled sturgeon spine or bear grease on the granite, leaving a relatively permanent signpost once the red pigment bonded to the rock. The full meaning may have been lost in time, but the image remains.

THE TEMPERATURE PLUMMETED and the next day we met up with Nate and Matty, the videographers, as they trekked down the Angleworm portage with pulk sleds, smaller sleds with raised sides and stiff rods attached to a hip belt. Nate had a fever and was quite fatigued, so the dogs took over pulling his sled back to camp. Nate was out of it for the first couple days he spent with us—though we couldn't determine if the cause was the cold medicine he was taking or the fever itself. He excused himself from filming at one point as we created a trail down the lake to travel on the next day. Later he told us that he had been hallucinating when he walked the half mile back to the tent and zipped himself into his sleeping bag.

North Hegman Lake pictographs

This was a tense time for us. Nate and Matt tried to capture our life in the wilderness as it was, but it didn't always feel unscripted. We moved camp when we ordinarily wouldn't have, for the sake of filming. We experienced the coldest temperatures of the winter and could have spent several days in relative comfort in our heated tent, sipping tea with the dogs contentedly bundled up, napping. Instead, we were fully exposed to the elements while on the move, carefully following our old tracks back to Gun. Traveling on a packed trail surrounded by undetectable slush is like being on an invisible bridge suspended over the slush. In 20 degrees below zero, slush was more than just a nuisance—it could have been lethal.

Any time Tina chewed a bootie off her paw, one of us had to remove mittens to replace it as quickly as possible and then spend the next fifteen minutes rewarming numb fingers. Yet there we were, repeatedly waiting for Nate and Matty to get into position before guiding the dogs and toboggans past.

Had we become so accustomed to being on our own that we couldn't

Plowing through deep slush

tolerate welcoming people into our lives and our tent? We stifled our frustrations around the guests and instead took them out on each other in the form of disagreements about how a toboggan was packed or when to feed the dogs. Our relationship suffered until we realized what we were doing. This short film would be a tool to reach many more people long after we had exited the Boundary Waters, so we were afraid of messing it up. Acknowledging that the source of stress was our desire to make the film perfect resulted in us acting like ourselves again.

Of course, once we relaxed, some of the best shots were created. The coldest night of the winter—27 degrees below zero—came when we were camped on Gun. Nate and Matty captured the sunrise the next morning as we took turns launching cups of boiling water into the air. Water vapor instantly froze and the frost crystals would hang in the still air: frozen fireworks at dawn.

After Nate and Matty departed we made our way back to Tin Can Mike. We skijored down to Range

Helping the dogs across a hilly portage

Lake to meet the J team—Joseph, Jacob, and Jeff Goldstein, plus Jason Zabokrtsky—as they dogsledded in for their seasonal visit and delivery of a resupply. They surprised us with a fresh pineapple, which Jacob carried in his coat, preventing it from freezing until we ate it that evening. That was the first and only pineapple we would experience during the year. But their visit didn't last as long as we had planned. We spent one full day with them, dogsledding from our camp on Tin Can Mike to Fourtown and hiking over the Billygoat portages. When we returned to camp, Jeff told us that Joseph had gotten sick and would need to leave—right away.

We were shocked, but had no time to fret. Instead we escorted them out, knowing their dog team would make better time if they had something to chase. Darkness and cold enveloped us as we traveled down the well-worn trail to Range Lake. Tina, Tank, and Acorn seemed to grasp the seriousness of the situation, putting their heads down and setting a fast pace. Once the sun passed below the western horizon, we flipped on our headlamps so the dogsledders wouldn't lose sight of us. A few minutes later we turned around to see the glow of

Jason's headlamp illuminating a cloud of frost crystals generated by the rapidly freezing breath and body heat of six sled dogs. We were pinpoints of light weaving through the darkness.

We parted ways with the Goldsteins and Jason, giving quick hugs before heading back toward camp. Joseph struggled to hold back tears as he said good-bye, and for the first time we saw his vulnerability. It was easy to see this bright, well-spoken, funny teenager as almost superhuman—enduring leukemia and chemotherapy all while working to protect his favorite place in the world from harm. As Tina, Tank, and Acorn pulled us back across Range Lake and down the narrow trail through the woods, we sobbed and raged against the unfairness of it. No one should have to endure what Joseph had. Any little hardship we encountered during the year paled in comparison. From this moment on we would think about him daily and draw strength and courage from the example he set.

WE EXPERIENCED A mid-February thaw. A light snowfall turned to sleet,

The Goldsteins arrive with a resupply

then rain, and our slushy world became even wetter. We had learned not to travel on days like this, so we brewed another round of coffee and settled into sedentary tent life. Acorn didn't seem to mind, contentedly curled up on her pad for hours on end. She would occasionally stretch, lap up some water from a puddle, spin in a circle, and settle back down. For the first time all winter, our ice hole didn't skim over. The air temperature was above freezing. Tendrils of fog wafted around the tent and obstructed our view of the nearby cliffs. Rapidly evaporating snow contributed to humidity in the air.

We decided to move once the forecast dropped to a 20 percent chance of precipitation. The dogs seemed to be glad to get a move on and so were we. A damp snow

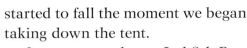

started to fall the moment we began taking down the tent.

As we emerged onto Jackfish Bay, numerous wolf and fox tracks left a record of comings and goings in the snow—a wilderness highway interchange of sorts. We traveled down the length of the bay in near whiteout conditions. Half the time our skis and dog paws plunged through the crust of snow and ice to several inches of water. The deepest slush puddles were made visible by dark drain holes, gray circles of open water ranging in size from dinner plate to manhole cover. The dogs clearly disliked wet feet as much as we did.

We opted to camp on land that night, given the soupy conditions on the lake. The dogs nestled in the woods, content in their dry jackets and on top of their pads. A big full moon rose above our bluff. The red lights of a giant cell tower gleamed across the bay, reminding us of our proximity to the edge of the Wilderness and the world of human habitation just outside.

After waiting out one more rainy day, we headed to Fall Lake to meet our fathers and several friends. A mile before reaching the Four-Mile

The whiteout lifts, revealing Jackfish Bay

WINTER

Portage a large dog team cruised across the bay in front of us and over the portage. Once our dogs turned onto the trail they were unstoppable. Their racing instincts kicked in, their ears perked up, and they took aim for the other team. They seemed overjoyed. What were their thoughts at that moment? Were they under the impression that we were in one big race and just now found our way back onto the racecourse—after losing the trail for weeks, plodding across trackless lakes in deep snow and slush, and camping alone night after night?

The next few days would be filled with visitors. Our fathers camped out for a few nights, along with our friends Don Watson and Neil Sherman. Don had been our coworker at Wintergreen for years. He had more winter camping experience than all of us combined, having spent years teaching and dogsledding in remote communities in Alaska. Neil, a plein air painter from Grand Marais, spent several days working behind his easel, with a brush held in his mitten, in and around our campsite.

Five men from the Twin Cities whom we had never met trekked out to deliver a resupply and film a story for Ron Schara's *Minnesota Bound* television show. They told us they'd heard that we really liked receiving fresh vegetables and fruit. Well, they said—handing us a grease-soaked paper bag of enormous donuts—they'd decided to go a different route. We each devoured one before inviting them to join us for a polar plunge. We had spent about an hour enlarging a hole in the ice, and it was an unseasonably warm day, with a high of 46 degrees—perfect for our monthly dip. Before we knew it, they were stripped down to their underwear, using our tent as a sauna and then taking a dunk.

The next day, we broke camp and met up with Sam Cook, the outdoors reporter for the *Duluth News Tribune*. He had interviewed us many times over the years, covering our Wilderness Classroom expeditions, and was excited to skijor with Acorn. By the time we emerged from the Four Mile Portage into Hoist Bay we had all stripped off layers and slathered on sunscreen. For the first time we were able to skate ski on an icy sun-warmed crust. We pitched camp on the ice near Beaver Island on Basswood Lake. Once we were settled in for the night, we began reminiscing and answering

Sam's interview questions. He is a skilled outdoorsman and it was a pleasure to get to know him better while basking in the warmth of our woodstove. Like us, Sam was drawn to this maze of lakes and rivers in his youth. He had carved out a life documenting the outdoor pursuits that help make this area so special.

We escorted Sam to the edge of the Wilderness the next day, each of us skijoring with a dog. Snow had started falling by the time we got to Newfound. Half a mile from the Wilderness boundary we saw three men with pulk sleds heading toward us. They were looking for us, and handed us a stack of dark chocolate bars as we exchanged greetings. Although we had never met before, they had been following our progress on social media and wanted to support our efforts. Sam chuckled as he scribbled notes and snapped photos of the chocolate delivery before saying goodbye.

Our monthly dip in the lake

We enjoyed all our visitors and realized that their passion for the Boundary Waters was critical to our long-term goal of permanently protecting the watershed from sulfide-ore copper mining. From donuts to chocolate bars to the simple gift of human company, we received a lot of support from friends and strangers alike. But we were ready to head deeper into the Wilderness again. We longed for the solitude and silence that engulfed camp when we were alone.

MORE WARM WEATHER made us realize we no longer needed our winter sleeping bags. The sun's rays were getting more powerful every day. Two bald eagles circled overhead in the early evening. How long would it be until they were tending eggs in their nest? As the sun set, we could hear them twittering, interspersed with the tooting of a northern saw-whet owl—not just practicing this time, but actively seeking a mate. Spring was not far off.

While camped on Newfound we built a snowman. Over subsequent days we watched it melt—shrinking, deforming, and eventually toppling over. All the snow on the lake melted, resulting in standing water over the ice. Eventually the water eroded the ice at key weak points and drain holes opened up. Like rainwater running into a sewer, the melted snow flowed toward these mysterious holes and swirled down to the lake below. Sticks, leaves, and other debris accumulated above the drain holes and organic matter was whipped into a fluffy brown foam. It was a sad scene. We love winter. Life is simple in the cold, distilled to the bare essentials. There is nothing like gliding across the frozen wilderness, an untracked blanket of white stretching to the horizon, the swish of skis, dogs panting, and your thumping heart the only sounds. It seemed as if winter had just begun—and now spring seemed to be arriving early. How would we ever say goodbye to the dogs? We didn't want the season to end.

Melting snowman on Newfound Lake

News from the outside world kept us in camp, glued to our little radio and email inboxes for a couple of days. On March 6, Governor Mark Dayton spoke up for the Boundary Waters. He sent a letter to the CEO of Twin Metals Minnesota:

As you know the BWCAW is a crown jewel in Minnesota and a national treasure. It is the most visited wilderness in the eastern U.S., and a magnificently unique assemblage of forest and waterbodies, an extraordinary legacy of wilderness adventure, and the home to iconic species like moose and wolves. I have an obligation to ensure it is not diminished in any way. Its uniqueness and fragility require that we exercise special care when we evaluate significant land use changes in the area, and I am unwilling to take risks with that Minnesota environmental icon.

Last Monday morning, I called the Director of the Bureau of Land Management (BLM) to discuss the importance of the BWCAW to Minnesotans. I apprised the Director of my strong opposition to mining in close proximity to the BWCAW. I was informed that the BLM is in the process of making a determination pertaining to the renewal of Twin Metals' federal lease holdings. I believe that the BLM decision will offer further guidance on the future of mining in the area.

In light of my concern about using state lands to advance mining operations in close proximity to the BWCAW and given the uncertainty surrounding Twin Metals' federal mineral leases, I wish to inform you that I have directed the Department of Natural Resources not to authorize or enter into any new state access agreements or lease agreements for mining operations on those state lands.

On March 8, Twin Metals was dealt another major blow as the Department of the Interior determined that the BLM did not need to automatically renew two expired mineral leases first issued in 1966, before the Clean Water Act existed. Stopping this renewal had been a major goal of the Campaign to Save the Boundary Waters from the very beginning. We had been fighting for it ever since we started planning Paddle to DC in 2013. Governor Dayton's action and the Department of the Interior's legal

Gathering water was a daily chore

opinion were huge steps toward protecting the Boundary Waters. We hugged, danced, and celebrated these announcements.

With this flurry of news we were mentally transported out of our campsite on Newfound to the state capitol and Washington, DC. We frantically posted on social media, wrote an article for the Campaign to Save the Boundary Waters, recorded video footage, and tried to absorb all the coverage. We took a photo of our melty snowman holding a sign that said "Thank you Governor Dayton. —From the BWCAW."

AFTER THE LAKE'S surface drained, travel conditions were ideal. We packed up camp and took off at a blistering pace down the Moose

Chain toward Knife Lake. The dogs pulled the load easily and the person at the back of the train gained a new task—preventing the toboggans from swerving out of control in a snaky version of crack-the-whip.

Daily we marveled at the amount of light gained and the increased intensity of the sun. The temperature dipped only a bit below freezing during the night and Knife Lake cracked and boomed as ice expanded and contracted. We were no longer tempted to stay curled in our sleeping bags waiting for the sun's first weak rays to kiss the tent walls. Instead we were up early, hoping to get going before the heat of the day. Frost quickly melted off the toboggans and any item that had been left outside overnight. Tree branches that had been coated in delicate white crystals just moments before began dripping. The dogs picked at their breakfast rather than quickly devouring it as they had done all winter.

We departed on an ambitious day trip out of the eastern half of Knife as a strong wind from the south pushed us along. We cruised on the glare ice past Thunder Point and up into the North Arm of Knife. Sparse snow hung on in the woods, but many rocky outcrops and patches of bare ground emerged on south-facing hillsides. The dogs gravitated to the shady shoreline, where they could get some traction in the thin layer of remaining snow. There we discovered a fresh dogsled track. Past the narrows, we saw two people out on the ice, fishing Knife's cold deep waters for lake trout. Their sled dogs began howling as we passed.

We made our way over a series of small lakes—Ottertrack, Gijikiki, Rivalry, Lake of the Clouds, Lunar, Cherry, Topaz, Amoeber, and back to Knife—connected by steep rocky portages that would be extremely difficult to navigate with a loaded toboggan or dogsled. We reveled in the solitude and remoteness. We saw no tracks or evidence that humans had visited this area since the lakes froze in the fall, though other animals were very vocal. The muffled silence of winter had been replaced almost overnight by the chatter of red squirrels, the distant pounding of pileated woodpeckers, and the calls of gray jays.

Midday brought the warmest temperatures since October, rising to the mid-fifties. We let the dogs loose on each portage and took off our skis to hike through the soft snow. As we made our way onto Lake of the Clouds, the heat of the sun radiated

WINTER

off the dark cliff face. For the first time in months, we sought out shade for our lunch spot, instead of sun and shelter from the wind. The surface of the lake took on the consistency of a melting snow cone and we stopped frequently so the dogs could eat snow or take a drink from open water. We had stripped off layers of clothing until we were in little more than our long underwear, but the dogs' coats had grown thick over the winter. They would begin shedding soon, but for the moment we had to watch them carefully to make sure they didn't overheat.

On Topaz what appeared to be a rock turned out to be a moose carcass slowly emerging from the melting ice. Its mottled purple-blue skin was stretched taut. Had it died before freeze-up? Had it fallen through the ice? In the sunlight, life seemed so placid and safe. The moose was a harsh and very real reminder of the dangers of thin ice and cold water, which were increasing with every passing day. Nature didn't care about us, and if we weren't careful we could suffer the same fate.

Hauling firewood on Knife Lake

Back at camp, we pulled our chairs from the tent and aired our bare feet, relishing the late-day sun. When it finally did get dark, a sliver of moon hung in the sky. It felt unfamiliar to experience a clear night that wasn't cold, and to not have to worry about staying warm. We had dedicated hours every day to the basic tasks of survival: gathering, cutting, and splitting firewood; chopping a water hole; and hauling water. Now we reveled in fewer chores and the simple pleasure of a warm breeze flowing across bare skin, something we would not have noticed if we had spent the winter insulated by a house.

By eight o'clock the next morning the sun was already blazing. We had a date on Snowbank Lake—visitors were coming—and we traveled down the length of Knife Lake quickly and efficiently, the dogs moving well in the cool morning air.

Dave took off his skis and jogged behind the toboggans on the winter portage into Ensign Lake. Feeling the sudden loss of forward momentum on the toboggan train, he looked up in time to see the dogs sprint away. The carabiner that attached the gangline to the front toboggan had caught on a tree root—we always used a locking carabiner, but had misplaced it just the day before. Without any resistance behind them, the dogs sprinted down the trail and out onto the lake. There was a well-worn dogsled trail for them to follow for twelve miles to the Moose Lake landing. But after several miles the dogs turned onto a little spur that led into a recently occupied campsite in a bay.

Dave threw on his skis and set off in pursuit of the dogs. He didn't stand a chance of catching them running at their top speed; he just hoped he could ski at a decent pace until they slowed down. He breathed a sigh of relief when he saw them veer off the main trail. Once he did finally catch up to the dogs, they had stopped to eat snow and sniff around the campsite.

With dogs and toboggans reunited, we made our way across a series of portages and water bodies. Exposed rock gouged the toboggans and we carefully skirted open water. The ice-covered expanse of Snowbank was a welcome sight. The distant shoreline shimmered as we worked our way across the ice. We were drenched in sweat and sunburned. Halfway across we saw several abandoned ice-fishing holes.

Without a second thought, we filled our water bottles and splashed our faces from one hole while the dogs lapped from another. We scooped slush into our baseball caps and plopped them back on our heads before trekking the remaining couple of miles to our campsite.

We were expecting several groups of visitors over the next few days: friends from Ely; Patagonia employees from Saint Paul and Chicago; a Wintergreen group; Land Tawney, from the nonprofit Backcountry Hunters & Anglers; the singer-songwriter Ben Weaver; Bill Deville, a DJ at the Current, a Minnesota Public Radio station; and others. Ben Weaver had contacted us out of the blue, wanting to contribute to the cause and raise awareness about the threat to the Boundary Waters through his music. He was coming to perform for us in our tent—a mini-concert in the Wilderness.

Visits like these were critical. For nearly six months we had been communicating with the outside world, but often these communications were one-way. The data fee on our satellite terminal was about five dollars a megabyte—approximately five hundred times more expensive than cell phone data—so for the most part we weren't logging onto Facebook, or reading comments on our Instagram feed. The information we received was limited to text-only emails from friends, family, and the Campaign to Save the Boundary Waters staff. This separation allowed us to focus on the wilderness around us, but we didn't always have a sense of our work's reception in the outside world.

Hearing from Ben and others boosted our spirits and gave us the energy and motivation to continue sharing our experiences. Our visitors told us how much they enjoyed listening to the weekly podcast and following us on Instagram, and how they were sharing our blog posts with their friends and encouraging people they knew to call their elected officials and take action to protect the Boundary Waters.

In limited contact with Ben prior to this visit, we had learned that he rides his bicycle to most of his performances. He would do the same now, riding from Ely to the Snowbank Lake landing. Since bikes aren't allowed in the Boundary Waters, he would meet Bill and a videographer, who would be documenting the visit for the Current, as well as Levi.

Unfortunately the four came in on the day winter returned with a vengeance. We hooked up the dogs to a little dogsled we were borrowing from Wintergreen and as we cruised close to the Wilderness boundary, the temperature dropped enough to shift the precipitation from rain to snow. Visibility dropped to a mile, and then to half a mile. The wind blew the snowflakes sideways and we tucked into an island campsite to wait for our visitors. The dogs stayed dry under the dense branches of balsam firs while we took turns serving as lookout in the elements.

As the four travelers emerged from the muddled white-gray of the blizzard our greeting was brief. Bill seemed the most shell-shocked, so we encouraged him to ride on the dogsled. Heading across a frozen lake in a whiteout took him out of his comfort zone, but challenges overcome out in the wilderness often lead to the best memories and lasting positive effects. We skied in front of the dogs, attempting to retrace our rapidly disappearing tracks back to the campsite. At one point we lost our tracks entirely, but

Crossing Snowbank Lake in the blizzard

could just barely make out a familiar point ahead. We kept land in sight the rest of the way to the camp and the others trickled in as we were detaching the dogs from the sled.

That night we all gathered in the tent and Ben began his performance. His lyrics left us mulling conservation, our role and responsibility as humans living on this planet, and our deep ties to the earth. He gave us pieces of raw copper that we could use as offerings, giving it back to the land during the rest of our journey. We went to bed that night with two lines from his song "Appaloosa" running through our heads: "If we listen to what the land is saying / It will tell us what it needs." And we returned, then and later, to parts of his poem, "Why Do We Ramble":

Why is it I ramble, for what do I seek?
With only enough food for a couple days,
yet I always manage to eat . . .
Why do I ramble you ask?

It is in defense of the quiet places,
the primitive voices only found in snow
*   fall,*
the corduroy of leaf litter, waterfall mist,
coyote tracks, and tadpoles swimming
in the rainwater of this map folded heart.

HEAVY FROST ON the tent indicated that it had been a cold night. We had relocated to Disappointment Lake. Our visitors were gone and we enjoyed the simple gift of lying in bed, wrapped in warm sleeping bags, watching the light slowly change. It was our anniversary; we had been married for six years. We talked about our dogsled wedding on a warm spring day, and how we had spent most of our anniversaries out in the wilderness, waking up in a tent. We never give each other presents, feeling as if we already have more stuff than we need—a feeling that likely comes from spending so much time living out of canoes, kayaks, or toboggans, where unnecessary items are a burden. Even outside the wilderness, we fight the clutter of random items that creep into our lives and have the potential to insulate us from the fundamental joys of existence. We decided that taking the day off would be a good way to note the occasion, and lounged on the rock ledge in our campsite.

In fact there was a lot to celebrate just two days after our anniversary.

Celebrating six months in the Wilderness

March 23 marked the halfway point of our year—and the spring equinox. Levi gave us individual cakes, each topped with a candle shaped like the number six. Throughout the year, he did a great job of supplying us with what we needed to document and share milestones like this. We ate the little cakes before dinner so we could get a photo in full daylight. The resulting post would be viewed and shared by thousands of people, further spreading the word about our journey, the Boundary Waters, and the urgent need for citizens to speak loudly for this quiet place.

A more raucous party was happening simultaneously at the Northgate Brewery in Minneapolis, where a packed house celebrated our halfway point. One of the greatest strengths of our partnership with the Campaign to Save the Boundary Waters was all the creative ways they wove A Year in the Wilderness into their daily operations and strategic planning. We recorded clips for their events, they drove traffic to our social media and blog posts, and together we worked on fundraising appeals and email blasts. We sent them a video message at Northgate—as virtual guests of honor—and received one in return.

Perhaps the longer days were actually the best reason to celebrate. We found ourselves spending much more time outside, doing chores with our gloves off. The dogs didn't want their jackets. Our tent warmed like a little greenhouse on sunny days, reducing our need for firewood. Little by little, life in the Wilderness was getting easier for us with each passing day. We left Disappointment Lake with loaded toboggans. Exposed rocks greeted us at the start of the five-mile winter route that meandered along a creek, through bogs, across small lakes, and over forested trails to Thomas Lake. The challenging travel conditions had made this normally well-used route impassable all winter. We would be the first party to traverse the entire route this year, and we braced ourselves for an alder-strewn tangle and thin ice.

The first mile was deceptively easy as we followed a recently made dogsled track, but then the tracks ended abruptly and we saw where the dog team had turned around. When our progress was halted by dense spruce and tamaracks, we took a minute to determine the path the frozen waterway took. We moved forward at a snail's pace, plowing through the thick alders, until we emerged on top of a beaver dam and dropped into a small open bog. From then on, a rhythm of sawing and grunting our way over land and cruising across icy bogs brought us to Thomas. A sense of accomplishment washed over us when we spotted the untracked expanse. Seasoned mushers with big dog teams had been turned back on this route all winter long. Once again we had entered a region that had been largely unvisited since the lakes began to freeze in early November. We relished the wildness surrounding us as we glided silently across Thomas and Fraser Lakes.

A couple days later, at our campsite on Fraser, we were surprised when Tina gave an excited bark. We poked our heads out of the tent

Gliding across untracked Fraser Lake

in time to see six skiers—including our friend and fellow guide Lynn Anne—cruise around the point to the north. They were following up on a text we'd sent, letting Lynn Anne know that we had opened up the trail to Thomas. These local skiers had started at Moose Lake. After reaching Knife Lake, they made the decision to go for the loop. Their full loop would take them over forty-two miles. We tried to supply them with food for the second half of their journey, but no one would accept anything more than filling water bottles at our ice hole. Later we would receive an email reporting that they made it home around 9:00 p.m.—fourteen hours of skiing in all—after multiple equipment failures. When Lynn Anne's binding broke, she determined that fixing it meant she wouldn't be able to remove it again, which apparently made for some tricky maneuvering on the portages.

The next day we traveled from Fraser to Knife, following the group's faint ski tracks in reverse. We were heading back to Knife, hoping it would be an equally good place to experience another seasonal transition. As the cloudy gray day gave way

Camp chores at dawn

to blue skies and sunshine, the ice and snow conditions were ideal for traveling. Along the shore of Gerund Lake, we realized that what looked like a cliff face was actually the portage trail to Ahmakose Lake. It took both of us and all three dogs to haul each toboggan individually up the steep slope. We cringed whenever the plastic toboggan grated against the sharp rocks.

As we were cruising across Kekekabic Lake, Acorn suddenly stopped and let loose a stream of bloody diarrhea. Horrified, we weren't sure whether the cause was stress from the heat, bacteria in something she had eaten, a parasite, or a combination of these factors. She was drinking water regularly, which we took to be a good sign—at least she wouldn't get dehydrated. We let her run loose, hoping that would reduce the stress on her system. We were within a couple miles of our intended campsite for the night, so we continued, keeping a close eye on her, ready to load her onto a toboggan if necessary.

After getting Acorn settled in the tent, we left a message for Frank and called Dr. Freking, the Ely veterinarian on call on Easter Sunday. She kindly calmed us down—even though we were calling at 8:00 p.m. on a holiday—and convinced us that we didn't need to evacuate Acorn immediately. In fact, she explained, red blood in vomit and diarrhea is much less alarming than if it were black. Acorn was most likely suffering from gastroenteritis, Dr. Freking said, instructing us to start her on the antibiotics in our dog first–aid kit.

We spent a day in camp to let Acorn recover. She was keeping water and even some food down, and she was much perkier. Still, we made plans with Frank to expedite the departure of Acorn and Tina from our team. We had hoped that these two could stay with us for another week or two, but it was important for Acorn to go to the vet to make sure there wasn't anything more serious going on. Tank would stay with us through ice-out—and through the summer, too, if he adapted to being a canoe dog.

Acorn was back to her energetic self when we skijored west with the dogs a few days later. The portages were bare in spots, so we removed our skis to walk over duff, dirt, and

Tina could never get enough affection

rock. Getting onto Ensign, we had to divert around open water. The air warmed as the sun climbed higher in the sky. We would travel more than twenty miles round-trip from our campsite on Knife to our rendezvous with Frank, but the lake conditions were ideal and we sped along effortlessly. Halfway down Ensign, we pulled over and gave the dogs hugs. It was hard to say good-bye, and we knew that when Frank arrived he would only be able to contain his team's frantic energy for a couple of minutes.

On Splash Lake Frank arrived in a frenzy of loud lunging dogs. Their energy rubbed off on Acorn, Tina, and Tank, who began barking with more enthusiasm than we had seen all winter. Frank set the snow hook long enough to embrace us and greet all three dogs, spending an extra minute with Tank and then hooking Acorn and Tina up to his team. The team fell silent when Frank said, "OK, dogs. Let's go." Tank barked for a minute as his family disappeared across the lake, but once we turned toward camp, he happily trotted back to Knife with us. It was just three of us now.

Alone under a star-filled sky

SPRING

The sun's intensity increased with each passing day. As the snow and ice diminished, the forest awoke. A walk in the woods was suddenly made richer by the scent of earth, duff, and pine needles—scents we hadn't realized we were missing all winter. Now we inhaled them deeply.

In December we had struggled to charge our batteries, even when skies were clear. Now they seemed to charge in minutes. Having an ample supply of power made our communications much easier. We felt newly charged, too. We hardly ever fired up the woodstove. And we could travel so much farther in daylight than we could in previous months.

It was time to reclaim our canoe. Unfortunately, the crew of volunteers that trekked into Newfound with the boat, dry suits, life jackets, and paddles chose a day that was neither warm nor sunny. In fact, the temperature stayed below freezing all day, and a heavy snow began around noon. It certainly didn't feel like spring.

We were optimistic that we'd be able to pull the canoe across the lakes as we had at the beginning of winter. But after we set it down on Splash and loaded it, we quickly realized our mistake. When it refused to budge more than a few feet, we sprinted back toward Newfound to catch the resupply crew, which was hauling both toboggans toward the Wilderness boundary. We sheepishly retrieved one, strapped the canoe securely on top, and dubbed it the canoe-boggan. This solution was odd-looking but functional, and not without precedent. *Trader, Tripper, Trapper,* Sydney Augustus Keighley's memoir about living in the bush in northern Manitoba during the first half of the twentieth century, includes a story about how he lashed his canoe upside down on his toboggan in the spring. When he encountered open water he would flip the whole thing over, push it into the water, and paddle. In the old days travel couldn't just stop during the freeze-up or the thaw.

We had to disassemble this rig a couple times to portage over rocky trails. We took turns carrying the canoe and a pack, or a pack with our skis attached, paddles in hand, towing the empty toboggan behind. This was just the start of the creative solutions we would have to come up with as the seasons changed. But overcoming such hurdles is one of the things we love about spending time in the Boundary Waters. There is nothing quite like the sense of accomplishment and confidence built by meeting a challenge in nature head-on. Some call this character-building. Others call it type II fun—as opposed to type I, when you're laughing and having a good time, type II is less enjoyable in the moment but more pleasurable to tell stories about after it's over.

We experienced plenty of type II fun as we trudged the thirteen miles back to camp, with the east wind blowing snowflakes in our faces. We walked the last mile in the dim blue twilight. The shoreline to our right became an amorphous black blob sometimes protruding and sometimes receding. We were all tired after twelve hours of travel, and Tank began veering for shore, looking for a place to bed down. As if his efforts to sideline our progress weren't enough, the snow increased in intensity. Visibility dropped and our load was increasingly hard to pull. The closer we got to camp, the more difficult our task became.

When we eventually reached camp, we unloaded our canoe-boggan in complete darkness. Lounging in the tent near midnight, our stomachs full of tuna noodle casserole, fresh apples, and homemade brownies, we experienced the second half of type II fun, laughing at ourselves for having hauled a loaded canoe

Hauling the canoe back to Knife Lake

through five inches of fresh snow. The circumstances made it easy to laugh. We had plenty of food and an eclectic assortment of winter and summer equipment: a canoe and a toboggan, paddles and skis, life jackets and down jackets. Whatever Mother Nature dished out as winter transitioned into spring, we would be ready and waiting.

BETWEEN SEASONS, WE also occasionally found ourselves between nature and civilization. On April 1, we filed our taxes from an exposed hilltop, making use of a weak cell signal. The wind numbed our fingers as we hurriedly plugged in numbers and kept an eye on the rapidly diminishing battery. The task felt distinctly absurd, in light of the fact that our survival depended on addressing much more physical, pressing needs: shelter, warmth, sustenance, clean water. It reminded us that our time in the Boundary Waters was temporary and that eventually we would have to return to the outside world, for better or worse.

The ice seemed to be hanging on, so we decided to trek east to Ottertrack Lake on April 5. When the snow stuck to our skis, we walked and took turns pulling the canoe-boggan with Tank. He had settled into his role as the sole dog, sleeping in the tent at night and lounging in the sun by day. Helping him pull the load gave us a new appreciation for the dogs' hard work. But Tank wasn't used to being a lead dog, and often veered off track, with his nose to the ground, when we crossed wolf, fox, or otter tracks. We quickly learned to say, "Tank, on by," in order to keep him focused on the task at hand.

Trekking down Ottertrack Lake

We set up camp on Ottertrack. Over the next week, the weather alternated between intense snowstorms and gorgeous sunshine. We resigned ourselves to time in camp, taking turns reading Farley Mowat books aloud for entertainment as a blizzard raged on outside. After nearly seven months in the Wilderness, it had become perfectly natural to let the weather dictate our activities. On an unpleasant day, why contemplate doing anything but settle in for another pot of coffee, read, and write in our journals? How lucky we were to be unencumbered by schedules, drifting with the seasons, present with each other.

On the next clear day we set out for Saganaga Lake. Saganaga had long been one of our favorite lakes in the Boundary Waters, thanks in part to the chapter titled "Farewell to Saganaga" in Sigurd Olson's *The Singing Wilderness*. "The lake was calm and its islands floated like battleships in a sea of crimson," he writes. "Far in the distance the loons called. This was Saganaga as it used to be. I loaded in my worn packs and pushed off toward the open sweep of the lake beyond Cache Bay. My paddle all but

sang as it dipped the blue-green water, and once more came the feeling of detachment I had known when I first came in many years before. Saganaga then was deep in the wilderness, a symbol of the primitive, perfect and untouched." A sense of familiarity and nostalgia grew as we wound our way through the western narrows and then caught our first view of the open expanse of lake. Unlike Olson, we had only known Saganaga long after its connection with civilization was established. But we could still see its grandeur despite the hum of motorboats and the entry-point parking lot just an hour away. We've spent plenty of time in more remote wilderness throughout North and South America, but while our perception of Saganaga's wildness has seen some wear and tear, the lake—like a worn childhood teddy bear—still holds a special place in our hearts.

We had paddled across Saganaga near the midpoint of the North American Odyssey, as we followed the Border Route. Bryan Hansel, our friend and a photographer from Grand Marais, had photographed us paddling past the golden tamaracks after the Monument portage at

Dave opens up the ice hole

the height of their fall brilliance, and again in the morning fog near the mouth of the Granite River. More recently, we'd paddled the lake on our way to Washington, DC. As we passed the entrance to Cache Bay, we remembered gazing at the pictographs tucked farther in as kids. On an island past American Point we set up our tent in a campsite where Amy had stayed with her family on one of her first canoe trips.

The rhythm of alternating weather continued and we spent another day stuck in camp as a strong northwest wind pummeled the tent. We read and listened to the radio—we were far enough east now that we could pick up WTIP, the Grand Marais community station. We enjoyed hearing the familiar voices of friends and avidly followed news about the towns along the edge of the Boundary Waters. We had seen lots of visitors, but we missed close connections with our community. In the Wilderness we couldn't invite friends over for dinner at the drop of a hat, or pick up the phone and call a loved one. In many ways these were small prices to pay for the enriching experiences we were blessed with and our ability to advocate for the Boundary Waters. Still, the sacrifice made us melancholy at times.

WE LEFT SAGANAGA and made a big push to reach Knife in one day. The sun beat down and our muscles protested, reminding us that a distance of thirty miles was more than we had demanded of our bodies all winter. We realized later that we made this effort because we were homesick—not for a house, but for our favorite campsite on Knife. Everything was changing all around us rapidly, and the towering red pines on the familiar rocky peninsula held the promise of comfort.

The next morning we woke up sweating with the tent baking in full sun. It took a minute for us to register the sounds that were erupting from the woods. A chorus of birds was singing. Birds! Where had they come from? Some were likely just passing through on their migration. Others were settling in for the season.

Overnight, it seemed, the forest had come alive.

It was unnervingly warm. We set out to complete a firewood-gathering mission before the lake surface got too sunbaked and soggy. Tank looked at us reproachfully as we slipped a harness over his head, taking his time to get up.

In the burned area to the northeast, we found a couple dry charred trees and cut them into eleven-foot pieces to load in the toboggan. We filmed the process, guessing it was probably our last such venture of the season.

By the time we walked back, the ice had become mushy near shore. Out toward the middle of the lake it was dry and dark, having recently drained. The ice had started to candle; the surface looked as though someone had carved an intricate labyrinth into it. Drain holes a foot in diameter were surrounded by grooves radiating outward like octopus tentacles. Our last measurement of the ice had indicated it was about a foot thick, but at this stage it begins to grow significantly weaker. We would need to tread lightly going forward.

The morning birdsong increased in intensity and variety with each passing day. Neither of us had ever

been much of a birder, but now we sat up on the hill above our campsite, listening and scouring the tree branches, poring over images and sounds in the Audubon bird guide app on our phone, and effectively learning a new language. Slowly we were able to identify the species harmonizing our morning wake-up call. The chickadees were singing a two-note song in addition to their usual "chick-a-dee-dee-dee." A nasal and repetitive "yank-yank" had been driving us crazy, because it was everywhere: when we finally saw a red-breasted nuthatch and could pair an image with the song, we were ecstatic. The twittering trill of the common redpoll. The high-pitched "wicka-wicka-wicka" of a northern flicker and the high "zer, zee, zer-zer-zee" of the black-throated green warbler. After a winter of quiet broken only by the familiar raven, gray jay, and chickadee, the birdsong that filled the air was exhilarating—as if a flood of new folks were moving into the neighborhood.

Other animals became more active, too. Red squirrels frequently scampered overhead in the tree branches, chattering away. On the top of Thunder Point a curious

chipmunk scurried right up to Tank, realized its mistake, and disappeared under a juniper bush.

Late one evening we walked down to the lake to fill our pot with water. Our headlamps caught a small shiny object moving through the duff. It was a salamander, slowly walking along. Soon we found another. They had dark skin with blue spots: blue-spotted salamanders. On our way back to the tent we saw two more. What were they up to? Snow had covered this path just three days ago, the lake was still largely covered in thick ice—and yet salamanders were out cruising the forest floor! A whole new world was being born before our eyes.

BY THE MIDDLE of April we were anxious to paddle. Knife was nowhere near open, but on an exploratory trip to Bonnie we found open water. Dressed in our dry suits, we made our way to the portage with Tank towing the canoe. Much of the lake was still covered in ice that was six inches thick, but we could paddle

A blue-spotted salamander

in a thin seam of open water along shore while Tank napped on land. After a lap, we decided it was time for his first canoe ride.

Wanting to ensure that he had a positive introduction to canoeing, we plied him with treats. Initially one of us had to hang onto Tank, constantly reminding him to sit, while the other paddled. But before long he turned his nose into the slight breeze created by our movement and assumed the position of a dog contentedly sticking its head out a car window. So far, so good, though we were a little nervous about more intensive paddling across frigid lakes. Fortunately, we had bonded tightly over the winter and knew Tank would trust us even when new experiences seemed scary.

Encouraged by our success, we decided to trek down to the Robbins Island narrows to look for more open water. On our way we passed a group of gulls perched on rocks, flying overhead, and even awkwardly waddling around on the ice. These gulls had been contributing to the raucous chatter we'd heard every morning since arriving back at our campsite. It was a challenge to keep Tank focused on our route and not on the new smells of the gull rookery.

At the narrows we decided that the best way to launch the canoe was directly off the ice. We coerced Tank into the boat with treats, assumed our positions standing next to the bow and stern seats, placed our hands on the gunnels, and began pushing the canoe toward the open water as we ran, hopping in just as the ice began to sag and the canoe slid into the water. And so we invented a new sport: Boundary Waters bobsledding. Once we were floating, Tank relaxed. Afterward we walked back to our campsite under the oppressively hot sun, excited by our newfound ability to move amphibiously over ice and water.

On a cooler cloudy day, we measured the thickness of the ice to the north of our campsite and found that it was still more than eight inches thick. We loved staying in one spot and watching the changes unfold around us, but our food supply was running low and we had scheduled a Skype call in a few days. With below-freezing temperatures in the forecast, we were less optimistic about ice-out. Weighing

Boundary Waters bobsledding

our options, we decided to move off Knife while it was safe to walk across the ice. We would travel through the smaller lakes to the south of Knife in order to reach Newfound the next day. We woke again to the warm brilliance of the sun on the tent, birds singing, and gulls squawking outside. Even though we were going to haul the canoe across the ice first, we packed as if we were paddling, to make sure there was room for us and the dog, along with all our gear and food. A bundle of skis protruded from the stern and small items were stuffed in every nook and cranny. The toboggan was wedged inside the canoe, lying flat along the bottom: canoe-boggan 2.0.

We hooked ourselves up along with Tank to haul the load, but he sped ahead of us, effortlessly pulling the loaded canoe—at least two hundred pounds—on his own. The ice had candled and drained, so there was barely any friction. Our solution was to take turns holding a rope attached at the back to slow Tank down. He reminded us of the little dog from *How the Grinch Stole Christmas!*, forced to pull the Grinch's sleigh all by himself. If we had tied an antler to Tank's

Tank hauling our loaded canoe

head it would have completed the picture.

As we set out, we heard the deep swoop of a large bird of prey passing directly overhead. A juvenile bald eagle flew low, its massive silhouette backlit by the pale morning sky and its head turned quizzically. We imagined our little train was a strange sight from above, especially at this time of year. The eagle flew ahead as if leading the way, exactly in the direction we needed to go.

Our first portage served as a real test for how to handle the eclectic assortment of gear—and we managed it in just two trips. We each carried a pack on the first trip, with skis or snowshoes and paddles in-hand, and then returned for two more packs and the canoe (with the toboggan left in it). Our first glimpse of Bonnie Lake left us stunned. A summery scene greeted us—shimmering open water, with a solo loon gliding gracefully across its surface.

We decided to film the process of loading the canoe. To get the angle we wanted we chose a somewhat precarious position for the camera, standing the tripod in about a foot of water, the lens pointed back at

shore. But as we struggled to wedge the last pack in, the canoe shifted. We heard the sound of a light tap on a hard surface, and then a plop as the tripod tipped over. After opening the camera up and dumping out the water, we wiped the exterior of its different components, packed it away, and continued on. In the end the lens was a total loss, but we were able to salvage the camera body by storing it in a bag of dry rice for forty-eight hours.

We managed to paddle across two-thirds of Bonnie before hitting a sheet of ice. Using our canoe as an icebreaker would have been easy enough, but Tank wriggled and tried to escape whenever the hull met ice. So we pulled over, dropped Tank on shore, opened up a channel, and then returned to pick up our bewildered companion.

Worn down and a bit discouraged, we made our way to Spoon Lake. There we fought our way across a small bay, with candle ice tinkling and shattering under the bow of the canoe. We followed a rhythm of propelling the front half of the canoe up onto the ice sheet, waiting for it to sag and eventually break. Around a

Paddling through candle ice on Spoon Lake

point another narrow band of water opened up along shore. We paddled until we ran into ice too solid to give way. Fortunately, we were near a campsite. The portage into Dix Lake lay just around the next point, but it might as well have been ten miles away. As a crow flies we were about a mile from our last campsite; we had only traveled some three miles overall, but we were exhausted.

Cooking breakfast in our tent on Spoon, we heard on the radio that Prince had died. People were flocking to Paisley Park in Chanhassen and First Avenue in Minneapolis while we sat listening to Prince's songs and sipping tea in our tent, in the rain, miles from the nearest road.

The ice on Spoon wouldn't release us. We spent several days watching it shift, sag, darken, and disappear. During the transition we ventured back to Thunder Point for a cell signal. If we'd reached Newfound, close to the edge of the Wilderness, we would have had a cell signal right in our campsite. But we were a long way from there, so we decided to double back, in the most marginal conditions of the entire year, in order to make a fifteen-minute Skype call. What was so important? The Outdoor Adventure Expo was happening at Midwest Mountaineering in Minneapolis, and Jason was presenting on the Campaign to Save the Boundary Waters and A Year in the Wilderness. We were supposed to call during the last few minutes of the presentation to say a few words and answer questions. We put on our dry suits and set out in the ever-widening lane of water between the shore and the ice sheet. The water was placid and the sun was shining. Tank sat in the bow, smiling and panting. Bonnie was now wide open—but on Knife we were forced to ram the ice, Boundary Waters bobsledding across the South Arm.

The combination of running and sliding was tiring for Dave and his feet occasionally punched through the ice, though his position straddling the stern would have kept him from falling in had it collapsed entirely. A lane of water appeared along the shore and we scooted over to it, paddling around the point to access the trail.

Several common grackles greeted us as we disembarked. We clambered up to Thunder Point in time to meet with a couple dozen people sitting in a classroom hundreds of miles away. For just a few minutes they had the opportunity to overlook Knife Lake in the midst of ice-out and we were

SPRING

reminded of what it was like to be surrounded by four walls and a crowd of people. We saw technology as a tool—just like a tent, stove, or paddle—that enabled us to share our experience and spur others to help protect the Wilderness. But as we made this call we were acutely aware that we were walking a fine line.

The last thing we'd want people to do on their own canoe trips is Skype with their friends. The wilderness provides a rare opportunity to unplug, slow down, and form real connections with nature. Sometimes it felt intrusive and odd to be making exceptions for ourselves, even though we knew it was in the service of a greater good.

THE OPEN WATER on Spoon gradually expanded. Daily we paddled as far as it would allow, relishing the destruction of the candle ice under the bow of our canoe. When we hit patches that were candled all the way through, we sliced through them like butter, freeing the vertical columns from their loose bonds. Leaving a path behind us of delicate icy debris, we got so into the

paddling that we cut through to a nearby set of islands. Then we traversed the length of the lake in a narrow seam of water. A loon couple fished in the seam, as well as half a dozen merganser pairs and one pair of much smaller buffleheads. The male mergansers were a rare sight; after breeding they would leave the females for the whole summer. How had these birds known the water would be open for them?

The next day dawned chilly and breezy. We let Tank out of the tent and set about starting a fire in the woodstove. Minutes later, Tank barked—something he never did. We sprang out of the tent, assuming he was in grave danger. The possibilities ran through our heads as we scrambled into our boots. Porcupine, bear, wolf? If he was tempted to chase a deer or a snowshoe hare, he might lose his way in the woods. But Tank came immediately after we whistled. Relief washed over us as we dug out a treat to reward him for coming so promptly.

Instead of sticking around, however, Tank ran down to the water's edge and began barking with renewed vigor. We followed and looked out at the lake, wondering if he'd spied a flock of birds. But there were no animals visible. The wind was blowing at a steady fifteen miles per hour, with occasional gusts, and the lake was completely ice-free. Apparently the wind had done in the last of the ice overnight. Several beaver-chewed sticks floated on the waves. Was he barking at them?

Tank kept barking and frantically running along shore, splashing his front paws and occasionally nipping at the surf. Suddenly it occurred to us that he was barking at the waves. This was the first time he had seen a lake not covered with ice. We both chuckled at the thought that a nine-year-old sled dog had never encountered open water. What did he think was causing the wave action? Was he imagining an animal thrashing below the surface?

We left him for a while as we made coffee and breakfast, expecting that he'd eventually tire himself out. But that didn't happen. Tank barked so much that he lost his voice and began squeaking instead. His front claws rapidly wore down from the rock shelf. He was soaking wet. So we led him out of sight of the water and tethered him to a tree with his makeshift leash. He continued to whine. Our amusement turned to

concern as we watched his frantic behavior. We tried various spots, thinking that maybe he'd forget about the water if he couldn't see or hear it. We tried giving him treats. We tried scolding him. In the end, the only way to mellow him out was to bring him in the tent. Even then, he looked at us wild-eyed and made efforts to get out. With the radio turned up and the stove radiating heat, he eventually curled up and fell asleep.

We were worried. If Tank grew this agitated every time he saw waves, there was no way we could keep him with us all summer. We were saddened by the thought of giving up our canine companion, but we also knew it would be wrong to keep Tank in a situation that continually stressed him out. Would he get used to open water? We would find out soon enough, when we paddled to Newfound.

On April 26 we paddled and portaged through nine lakes and didn't see any ice at all. Was Knife still partly frozen? We thought it probably was. But two days of rain and strong winds had been the final nail in the coffin for the ice on all but the deepest lakes, and the sunny days that followed would take care of the rest. We wore our dry suits, not

Spring made life easy

quite confident that the dog wouldn't capsize us in the dangerously cold water, but the day warmed up to the mid-sixties, and we were overheated by the end of it.

When we reached our campsite on Newfound, Tank's enthusiasm about the familiarity of our chosen campsite reflected our own feelings. He ran around sniffing until finally lying down to nap in the sun. We took advantage of the last daylight by sorting our gear. Many items that had once been necessary for our survival and transportation—skis and ski boots, our big saw, additional warm layers, ice picks—were now dead weight and could be jettisoned. We pitched our tent on the bare ground and fell asleep to the tooting of a northern saw-whet owl.

Having spent a month without seeing anyone else, we were eager to greet our visitors the next day. Soon after their canoes appeared, our campsite was full of laughter and conversation. When they departed, they took our winter gear, leaving us ready to travel light. A second group of friends came to

see us the next day. Lindsey Lang, who had supplied us with delicious dehydrated meals throughout the winter, brought a whole roasted chicken, still warm and wrapped in a tinfoil swan. With roasted vegetables, salad, and a small box of white wine, she had replicated a restaurant dining experience in the woods.

Alone again, completely satiated, and with streamlined gear, we experimented with setting up our new shelter. The Cooke Custom Sewing Lean was a tarp tent with no poles or floor and a mosquito-mesh front. It would be our cooking zone when the bugs were bad for the time being, and our only tent later in the summer. We appreciated the view through the screen and how much light filtered through the white silnylon. We came to think of it as a portable porch.

We made a move to Snowbank Lake and relished our greater portaging efficiency. Tank helped, too, carrying some of his food in newly acquired dog packs. In our new campsite we cooked dinner outside on a BioLite, our go-to stove from then on. It is fundamentally a stick stove with a built-in fan, so

we didn't need to carry fuel with us. We became experts at cutting and splitting pieces of wood that were four inches long and no thicker than one's thumb. We imagined that someone who came upon these miniature logs would think either that we were obsessive about processing wood or that a tiny lumberjack had been through the site. As we cooked, American redstarts flitted in and out of the surrounding pine branches, serenading us with their high-pitched whistling calls.

We stayed out late into the evening, enjoying the birdsong, the smell of red pine and duff, and the soft glow of the sun setting across the lake.

On the first day of May we left Snowbank and met Steve and Nancy Piragis on Parent Lake. We talked about the winter, observed the nearby birds, and ate smoked salmon, cheese, and crackers, along with olives and homemade pickles. They introduced us to birds we didn't yet recognize—warblers, vireos, and finches—and our world expanded a bit more. It was late by the time we hopped into our respective canoes.

Watching the sun set over Alice Lake

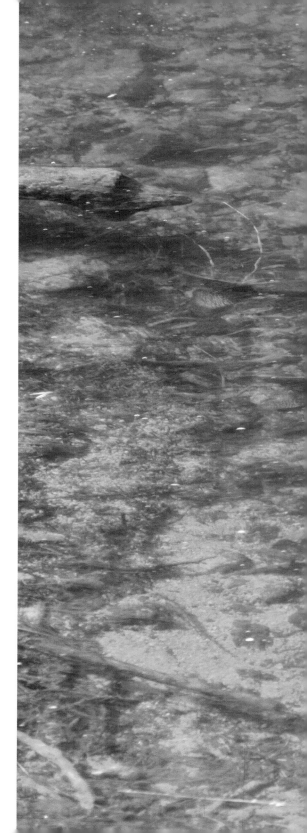

They headed back to the portage into Snowbank and we veered away to do water testing. When we finished we decided to stay at the campsite we had just left. Why not eat more food, lighten our load, and get an early start the next day?

THE FOLLOWING MORNING we decided to head south in order to visit new lakes. We would follow Drumstick Creek out of Parent, which we had only done once, years ago, in the winter. Not being an established travel route, we expected it to be challenging.

Luckily, the water was high, making the creeks and smaller lakes relatively easy to paddle. Poking around in the woods wasn't as difficult as it could have been, because leaves and underbrush hadn't emerged yet. Peering down into the shallow creek, it became apparent that the mucky bottom was no longer devoid of life. Shoots from lilypads were poking up, growing toward the newly available light. Late in the day we arrived at Lake Four.

Suckers spawning in the shallows

SPRING

While cooking dinner that evening, we noticed an object not much bigger than a quarter moving near our feet. Closer inspection revealed it to be a baby painted turtle, also called a northern slider. Wasn't it early for this small creature to be out and about? A white speck on its nose was a horn of sorts that it had used to escape from its eggshell. What odds did it have of surviving?

We spent some time paddling in the area burned by the Pagami Creek Wildfire, charred trunks scattered on the hillsides like giant pick-up sticks. We passed through Hudson and Insula Lakes, to Alice Lake. The purple petals of violets emerged from the cracks of buff-gray rocks. Mergansers, buffleheads, gulls, and loons became commonplace.

We packed up and departed Alice one morning, just as a southwest wind began to rile the lake's surface. We didn't have far to go before our first portage, on the Kawishiwi River.

As the roar of rapids increased, young men loading aluminum canoes along the riverbank came into view. They greeted us as we landed just downstream, and Tank was

Tiny turtle

showered with attention. This group was from the Voyageur Outward Bound School, on their nineteenth day in the Wilderness. When their leader asked us how many days we had been out, we said 227. Eyebrows raised across the group.

On Fishdance Lake we veered off the route to visit pictographs. One image remained in our thoughts for the rest of the day—an elliptical blob with vertical lines though it, like an eye with lashes. In light of the charred landscape we had just paddled through, we theorized that this could be an illustration of a burned island, the vertical lines representing tree trunks and their reflections in calm water. We felt as if spending time in the same forests and on the same lakes as the people who had created these images hundreds of years ago gave us a little more insight into how they perceived their world. We wouldn't presume that our experience was anything like theirs—we paddled a Kevlar canoe, slept in a nylon shelter, and ate mostly food that was brought to us—but we could venture interpretations of some images simply because they seemed to

SPRING

depict the environment we were currently immersed in.

Based on the images we'd seen scattered throughout the Boundary Waters—of animals roaming the forest and constellations in the night sky—we knew their creators had keenly observed the world around them. Perhaps if we all paid closer attention to the natural world, we would see more than resources to be extracted and harvested for material gain. We might even develop a greater understanding of the delicate framework that sustains all life.

We could have spent all day looking at these images, wondering about their origins, their creators, and their significance. But the wind blew us on. Near the next portage a bald eagle swooped down to the water. It stayed low, settling on a rock ledge. Had it caught a fish? Suckers were spawning above a nearby set of rapids. Eight of them swam against the current in shallow sunlit water. Moose droppings on one portage gave us some hope of a sighting. Old wolf scat was abundant on another. Yellow and black feathers

Fishdance Lake pictographs

SPRING

marked the spot where a predator had nabbed a goldfinch.

The remaining portages toward Makwa Lake were marshy, and we were overwhelmed by the calls of spring peeper frogs ringing in our ears.

As the sun dipped lower in the sky, the air became hazy. Eventually our eyes started to itch. We had heard on the radio a few days before that smoke from a forest fire thirteen hundred miles away—near Fort McMurray, Alberta—was heading in our direction. The air brought back memories of the fires we'd witnessed in the Boundary Waters: the Pagami Creek Wildfire, the Ham Lake Fire, the Cavity Lake Fire. These fires, as well as the 1999 Blowdown, had certainly altered the forest temporarily and we had felt the loss of massive red and white pines. Favorite campsites would never be the same. However, the forest was already recovering from the damage these natural events had inflicted.

A sense of relief settled in as we completed our last portage and dropped down onto Makwa. It was just a short paddle to a campsite

beneath the most stunning set of cliffs either of us had ever seen in the Boundary Waters. A wedge of black-and-white-striped rock rose to a height of fifty feet. The calm water reflected the stripes perfectly, doubling the appearance of their height. A loon couple cruised by our campsite as we prepared dinner.

At dawn a blanket of fog coated Makwa Lake so thickly that we could barely see the tiny island 50 yards from our tent. Residual smoke scented the humid air and obscured the sun, causing a diffuse pink-orange light that filtered through the fog. The gnarled jack pine out on the point was perfectly silhouetted. We took some pictures and video while boiling water for coffee, then ate granola with powdered milk as we listened to the radio. Eighty thousand people had been evacuated from Fort McMurray, due to the massive fire. There were also fires near Hoyt Lakes and Bemidji in Minnesota.

The next day we headed east. As we paddled through a portion of forest along Little Saganaga Lake that had burned about ten years

Smoke and fog on Makwa Lake

earlier, we glimpsed movement. A moose was chewing on new growth along the shore. While we were excited to see our first moose since November, we were saddened by the state of this skinny and nearly bald specimen. Its entire front half was gray and virtually hairless. No doubt this moose had damaged its coat in a futile attempt to rub off ticks. The unhealthy animal continued munching and slowly wandered up the bank as we drifted by.

According to the Minnesota DNR, the state's moose population has dropped by half since 2006, to about four thousand. Our glimpse of this moose suggested one of the reasons: milder winters result in more ticks in their coats. But they are also increasingly suffering from a brain worm that is carried by whitetail deer, and warmer summers are inducing heat stress. We wondered how the moose near the Kawishiwi River and Birch Lake would be affected by habitat fragmentation and noise from the proposed Twin Metals mine. An industrial mining zone in their forest would certainly be one more stressor for this already vulnerable population.

On the next portage, the smell

Scraggly moose

of moose permeated the air. The tamarack branches were coated in mint-green bundles of needles emerging from buds. We followed the meandering course of the Frost River, paddling against the current. A handful of lily pads had reached the surface and begun to unfurl. A pair of wood ducks floated past, the female looking rather drab next to its elaborately colored mate.

The next day we reached Cherokee Lake and aimed right for our favorite island campsite, but as we neared the site a tent came into view, along with a family going about their evening camp chores. We were no longer alone in the Wilderness. After shrugging off our astonishment, we made our way to a second-favorite campsite, which we shared with an uncommonly tame spruce grouse.

OVER THE FALL and winter we had spent more time than expected in the western half of the Boundary Waters, but now we were heading east. A contingent of our Cook County friends paddled in to see us,

bringing a delicious feast and stories from the past seven months. Sitting around the campfire well into the night, talking and laughing, signaled the beginning of the paddling season for us. We'd soon become accustomed to canoes drifting across lakes, occupied campsites, and exchanging greetings on portage trails.

Saying good-bye the next morning was difficult, but our friends had to go to work and we had a schedule to keep. On our way to Kelly Lake, downed trees littered the portages and our progress was temporarily halted by a dense tangle of bent and broken alders. We took turns cutting a tunnel big enough to get the canoe through. The next day, as we headed up the Temperance River through Jack and Weird Lakes, we spotted several moose grazing along shore. One was visibly smaller, a yearling. Each of them had healthy, dark brown coats. It was heartening to see that not all the moose in the Boundary Waters were as unhealthy as the last one we'd seen.

On May 15, the Minnesota fishing opener, we awoke to a dusting of snow and a cold northwest wind that stung our faces. A few hearty

Moose on Kelly Lake

souls plied the riled water with their paddles and wet lines, eager to catch walleye. We didn't bother. It seemed like a good day to build a fire in the woodstove and brew another pot of tea. The birds we had been seeing must have hunkered down too. We couldn't hear anything other than the wind rustling the tree branches.

The sun kept rising earlier and earlier and we began going to bed just before dusk, hoping to avoid the rapidly increasing mosquitoes. We had seen just a few of them on warmer evenings, and their bites reminded us that we had no desire to contend with swarms. We were grateful for our bug shirts and screened tarp shelter.

We portaged from South Temperance Lake to Brule Lake late one day, as the sun cast long shadows and began its golden hour. Looking out at Brule, we were astounded by its calmness. We were as close to home as we would get that year—we owned property just a few miles to the south—and we were intimately familiar with the lake's moods. On a lake eight miles long and one mile wide, this glassy stillness was rare. With no more than an exchange of

Greeting another beautiful day

glances, we aimed our canoe right down the center of the lake.

The only disturbance to the lake's placid surface was the V trailing behind our canoe and the rhythmic dipping of our paddle blades. We kept going well after the sun had disappeared behind us and purple gave way to inky blue ahead. As we sidled up to an island campsite, we had just enough light to unload and set up our tent before we needed headlamps. The first pinpricks of stars emerged while we cooked dinner and Tank chose his bed under an impressive white pine. After camping beside small lakes for so long, we had almost forgotten the freedom afforded by the big ones. Just off the point, loons dove, splashed, rose up, and flapped their wings, their reedy tremolos filling every corner of the vastness.

The morning gave us an opportunity to explore where we had landed. Brule was so familiar to us. We had guided numerous day and overnight trips here, practiced rolling our kayaks on its waters before circumnavigating Lake Superior, and even visited it as kids. We could picture the entry point's gravel beach landing and parking lot a short paddle away, followed by the couple miles that we had driven, walked, ridden bikes, and even dogsledded on many times. But imagining our place was almost as satisfying as actually going there, and the small wave of nostalgia passed nearly as quickly as it had come. As we sipped coffee on the rocky point that morning, a small buzzing object whizzed past our heads. We followed the sound, catching sight of a ruby-throated hummingbird, and wondered how much nectar it would find so early in the season.

Water exits the lake at two locations: at the northwest end, flowing into South Temperance Lake, and at the east end, flowing into Vernon Lake. In all our travels throughout North America, we've seen just a few lakes that have two outlets. How remarkable that water can take such varied journeys from Brule to Lake Superior. Water flowing west enters the Temperance River, before eventually reaching Lake Superior near Tofte. Water flowing east enters the Brule River and tumbles into Superior forty miles to the northeast, near Naniboujou Lodge. And raindrops falling just a few miles north of Brule take an entirely different path, to the Arctic Ocean. This split is thanks to the Laurentian Divide, which winds its way through the Boundary Waters. Rain that falls on the north side of the divide is in the Rainy River Watershed, leading north to Hudson Bay. Rain that falls on the south side flows toward Lake Superior and the Great Lakes Watershed, eventually making its way east to the Atlantic Ocean. The state of Minnesota is also at the top of a third major watershed: the Mississippi, flowing into the Gulf of Mexico.

One evening the sky darkened as thick thunderheads rolled in an hour before sunset. The wind had been blowing all day, pinning us to our campsite, and now deep rumbling began to the north of us. We climbed into our tent as flashes of light illuminated the clouds to the north. Just before a downpour started, Tank woke us up with a whine and scampered into the tent. How had he known to seek shelter before the first drops fell? We sat up for a while as rain pummeled the tent and the thunder grew louder.

Another day we sat on a sun-baked slope of rock, ten feet from the water's edge, watching the morning light dance off the water. A loon couple fished nearby. One was so close that we heard the droplets slide off its waterproof feathers as it emerged from the depths. It looked at us, plunged its head into the water to take another look for fish, and silently dove again.

THE BLACK FLIES were out in force as we headed to Winchell Lake. We passed a group portaging in the opposite direction and pitied their exposed ankles and arms, but they were smiling and happy, seemingly unfazed by the clouds of black flies lurking in the woods. We might have looked goofy in our bug shirts, with our hoods up and dark mesh covering our faces, but we were content to remain free of bug bites.

On Winchell we had our pick of south-facing campsites. We chose one with a balcony-like protuberance of rock set high above the water, from which we looked across the lake at rolling hills that had been burnt in 1995. The new growth was

Tank never tired of affection

now leafing out in bright yellow-green, with patches of darker green where conifers still stood. We could have settled in there for a long while, lazing days away and taking in the commanding views to the east and west, but the days were growing longer and the weather was warming—perfect for traveling. Even in the wilderness, it was impossible to avoid the 2016 presidential campaign entirely. Spotting Trump and Little Trump Lakes on our map, we thought a visit to them might be notable, though we couldn't find a lake named Hillary or Bernie. Unfortunately, the draw between Pup and Little Trump was an impassable tangle of alders. After twenty minutes of struggle we had advanced no more than a hundred yards, so we cut our losses.

Although we didn't succeed in reaching our goal, the trip was rewarding. The portage into Pup was seldom used and we had to feel our way through, looking for old cut marks. Partway in, we trudged through a bog filled with northern pitcher plants. This carnivorous plant holds a certain fascination for us. It grows in soil low in nutrients and so depends on obtaining nitrogen and phosphorus from insects.

Its deep pitcher-shaped leaves contain a pool of rainwater and downward-pointing hairs, which prevent its unsuspecting prey from climbing out.

In this bog we stumbled upon the mother of all pitcher plants, more than a foot in diameter. A tall stem protruded from the center of a bullseye. Numerous pitchers formed layer upon layer of concentric rings, and the spongy ground was carpeted in an elaborate pattern of the green and purple plants. Was this mass of pitchers one plant or many? If the former, how old was it? We didn't stay long to ponder these questions—the black flies caught up to us—but it was like nothing we had seen before.

We entertained a steady stream of visitors at a new site, on Horseshoe Lake. Several groups had offered to drop off a resupply, so Levi fit them into our schedule, one after another, each spending a night with us. From one group we requested burgers and french fries from the restaurant at Trail Center Lodge, which was on the way to their entry point. We devoured the food without bothering to reheat it. Paying for our burgers was the first and only time we would handle cash for a whole year. We had been carrying two hundred dollars packed with our IDs ever since we entered the Boundary Waters, but had no other occasion to use it.

We were about to canoe with another resupply crew to the Gaskin Lake portage when we noticed several dragonflies attached to the boat's sides. Their legs clung to what looked like other bugs, so we assumed they were eating something. Upon closer inspection, we realized that they had just undergone metamorphosis. They had recently emerged from their nymph exoskeletons and were hanging off our canoes, drying out and stretching their wings.

Suddenly, everyone was engrossed, taking pictures and delicately transplanting these vulnerable creatures to nearby rocks and vegetation. One of nature's many little miracles had instantly turned six adults into wonderstruck kids. The only actual child in the bunch, ten-month-old Jasper—our youngest overnight visitor all year—was also transfixed.

Dragonfly hatching

Over the next few days we watched this metamorphosis unfold multiple times. Initially a large, primordial-looking nymph—the form that a dragonfly spends most of its life in, creeping along the lake bottom—emerged from the water and moved upward. "They look like little monsters," one visitor observed.

They would settle in a spot with a slight overhang, firmly latched on, so their new bodies could take advantage of gravity. That was why the side of our overturned canoe made an optimal surface. They also clung to the trunks of cedar trees, balsam branches, rocks, and the guy lines for our tent.

First the head and legs emerged. Then the dragonfly would shift position to allow its wings to hang down. The wings were barely noticeable in the beginning, plastered to its body. Slowly they appeared to grow. The dragonfly's abdomen seemed to grow too, emerging wide and stubby, then slowly lengthening and narrowing. Eventually the dragonfly spread its wings for some final drying in the sun and breeze.

After cheering for these marvelous creatures for hours as they sat motionless, we held our breaths when they took to the air. We were devastated when cedar waxwings swooped overhead and snapped some of them up a few seconds after taking flight.

When we weren't transfixed by the dragonflies, we made several trips to explore the surrounding lakes and gather water-quality data. Returning to Horseshoe, we were hugging the shore when we caught a glimpse of a large brown body several yards ahead. We veered out to give a wide berth to a mother moose and calf wading in the water. The mother munched on aquatic vegetation, stocking up on nutrients to feed her young one, as we silently glided by.

Watching the dragonflies hatch, the moose feed in the shallows, and the effervescence of spring unfold around us, we were reminded of how important clean water is to the Boundary Waters ecosystem. We thought about this every day, when we filled our pots or dipped our cups in the lake for a cool drink. But when humans are insulated from the world—by cars, houses, light switches, and water faucets—it can be easy to forget that we are a part of nature, and that clean air and water are essential for us as well.

ON THE SECOND to last day in May, Frank and Sherri Moe paddled in for a lunchtime visit. Tank's ears perked up the moment he heard Sherri's greeting, and once they were on shore, there was a beautiful reunion. Tank stood on his hind legs with his front paws anchored on Frank's torso, planting sloppy kisses on both his owners' faces.

When it was time for Frank and Sherri to depart, we paddled with them for a while. Tank seemed to be showing off his new skills as a canoe dog, eagerly hopping in the canoe and sitting at attention. We could tell that they missed Tank, but we also knew that they cared deeply about the Boundary Waters. Letting us borrow Tank was one way to help effect change, and Frank and Sherri were proud that Tank was the star of our trio.

WE LEFT HORSESHOE and made our way west. Several long wet days passed. We caught a glimpse of bright sun, but nearly constant rain kept us soaked. Many of the portages were flooded with several inches of water, making it hard to find footing on slippery rocks.

Our slight grumpiness melted away, however, as we launched our canoe and saw two dark shapes moving through the mist in front of us. It took a minute for us to make out the heads of two moose—a cow and a calf—swimming in the lake, a small wake trailing behind them.

On Snipe Lake we found a campsite tucked away from both the main travel route and a strong northwest wind. The trees were spaced far apart, so we extended our guy lines and strung up a spiderweb of parachute cord. A flat slab of rock high over the water was an ideal spot from which to survey our surroundings. The sun reappeared the next day, and by the afternoon, nearly every piece of clothing we owned was laundered and hanging from the guy lines. Our spirits soared with the improvement in weather and we took comfort knowing we'd have clean dry clothes for the first time in weeks.

The next day we paddled onto the smooth expanse of Gillis Lake as the sun dropped toward the horizon.

Its cold clear waters were teeming with lake trout, so we cast a line and slowly trolled across. Sure enough, the rod doubled over within minutes. With a hundred feet of water beneath us, we knew we hadn't snagged a rock. A streak of silver rushed under the canoe as we reeled in the line, and soon a sixteen-inch lake trout lay on the boat's bottom. A beautiful south-facing campsite offered the perfect setting for a fresh fish dinner while watching the sunset.

On a warm sunny day—the first that began to feel like summer—we headed toward Gabimichigami Lake. A handful of mosquitoes droned in the darkest recesses of the woods early in the day, but they soon disappeared and we strutted down the portage trails confidently, bare-armed in T-shirts for the first time since we'd entered the Boundary Waters.

We stopped for lunch on West Fern Lake, at a campsite that looked like it didn't see much use. This site provided an ideal spot to park at the water's edge and take our first enjoyable swim since October.

We ate lunch as the sun evaporated the water off our skin. Two moose—a cow and calf again—were also swimming. They dunked in, clambered out, and shook a spray of glistening water droplets before disappearing into the shade of the pines. Had they been cooling off, too?

We visited several other lakes before looping back toward Gillis. A splash of brilliant turquoise—the color of a tarnished penny or the patina on the Statue of Liberty—stood out against a brown-gray cliff face, about fifteen feet up. We decided to investigate. Seeping water spread the color over the irregular surface of the lichen-covered rock. At its largest, the turquoise covered maybe a foot and a half square; in other places, just a blue-green line was visible. Was copper the source of this color? A geologist friend later suggested it was, in the form of malachite.

It was poignant and peculiar to suddenly see in the wild the mineral we were trying to keep in the ground. But we knew that what enters the Boundary Waters via natural seepage is minuscule compared to what could leach into the Wilderness if millions of tons of this rock were dug up, pulverized, and exposed to air and water.

A streak of turquoise caught our attention

The next day, heat and a lack of bugs had us stripped down to T-shirts again, as we made our way across Bat, Green, and Flying Lakes. New colors appeared throughout the landscape—blue flag irises near shore, pink wild roses and white bunchberry on the portages, while the white flowers of Labrador tea and the deep purply-maroon of pitcher plants adorned the bogs. After admiring the delicate pink of several lady's slippers on our way to Gotter Lake, the temperature dropped and the sun disappeared behind a blanket of roiling clouds. A loon called, heralding the impending storm, and thunder rumbled as we quickly made our way to the Brant portage. We hauled the canoe on shore just as heavy raindrops began to fall, soaking us instantly. Tank ran for cover and we had to coax him out of the underbrush and put on his leash. The cold driving rain provided a sense of relief from the oppressive heat we had endured just moments before. Lightning streaked across the sky overhead, from cloud to cloud. For a brief moment hail pelted us, and rain drummed on our heads as

Lady's slipper

well as the leaves above us as we walked. Rivulets formed on the steeper parts of the trail; the water was arriving too quickly for the soil to absorb. The storm rumbled past and the rain stopped as we took in the view of Brant Lake and then headed back to Gillis. A disheartening sight greeted us in camp. The wind had reversed during the storm, blowing directly into the screen side of our shelter, catching it like a windsock, and ripping up most of the stakes along two edges. Our sleeping bags were soggy and our pads had collected water. One chair had a puddle in the seat—where we had left one of our batteries. We pulled the dripping battery out of the puddle and grimaced. Despite all our wilderness travel experience, we were not immune to silly mistakes. Our demolished campsite served as a humbling reminder of nature's power. All we could do was laugh, hang our sleeping bags up to dry, and learn a lesson for next time.

Morning paddle on Snipe Lake

A NORTHWEST WIND blew us back toward Snipe. That evening a Swainson's thrush serenaded us with its reedy song as the wind dropped, and in the morning a song sparrow woke us. Musicians of the human sort came to visit, too: the singer-songwriter Jerry Vandiver, from Nashville; Eric Frost, a friend and cofounder of the Wilderness Classroom, and a singer-songwriter himself; Jerry's fiddle player, Amberly Rosen. We were going to finish a song that Eric and Jerry had begun, about our year in the Boundary Waters:

"This Quiet Place"
By Jerry Vandiver, Eric Frost, and Amy and Dave Freeman

This stream that flows so clearly
And seems to know how dearly
Each turn, each tumble, each drop so
*   humble*
Each sparkle of light gives its gift of life

To this lake that only wants us to listen
To the fate of its endless mission
Unspoiled, unchanging, yet always
*   rearranging*
From winter's deep cold to the beauty
*   that holds*

The birch, cedar, white pine, and spruce
That whisper a timeless chorus
With their deep and far-reaching roots
That echo the steps of all those before us

This ground that lies so sacred
And sound as it awaits us
We shoulder its fate
Preservation for all generations
Standing proudly, we must speak loudly
For this place, this quiet place
This quiet place.

Undeterred by our presence, a painted turtle clambered up from the water's edge. Over the course of a couple hours she found her ideal spot, dug a hole in the gravel bank, deposited and buried her eggs, and slowly made her way back down to the water while we finished the song.

As we said good-bye to the music crew, Nate and Matty returned for a third and final visit to help document A Year in the Wilderness. We jumped off cliffs on Cherokee Lake over and over, relishing the moment our bodies hurtled through space before making contact with the cool water. A moment of exhilaration passed as we propelled ourselves past Matty, at the top of the

cliff, and plummeted toward Nate, in the water.

Once we shot up to the surface and reoriented ourselves, we waited to hear the all-too-familiar phrase from Nate or Matty: "That was great! Let's do it one more time." What a contrast from the last time they'd been here, in the coldest week of the winter! Now they joined us as witnesses to the warm sunshine, with the deciduous trees fully leafed and wildflowers blooming in the woods.

That evening we tuned in to WTIP, because Jerry and Amberly were debuting and discussing "This Quiet Place." We were giddy as they began playing. By the end of the song, tears streamed down our cheeks. We were humbled by the creative actions being taken by people who care deeply about the Boundary Waters.

On the day after the summer solstice, our alarms beeped at 4:45 a.m. We were going for a sunrise paddle with Nate and Matty, to capture the ethereal moment as the morning fog burned off and the sun rose higher in the sky. Although Tank was an early riser, he sleepily blinked at us when we called him. By the third call he

A painted turtle laying eggs

knew we meant business, so he trotted down to the water's edge and
assumed his position in the canoe.

We glided effortlessly through
the golden halo of fog rising from
the lake's glassy surface and floated
on the brink of a narrow passageway
between two islands, ready to pass
through when the light was just right.
Rays of sun streamed through the
channel and Matty gave the signal
to paddle. We marveled at how the
light made the moss-covered rocks
glow. A loon popped up and the full
moon hung above the trees. Sigurd
Olson often referred to the Boundary
Waters as the "Singing Wilderness."
That morning the Wilderness was
singing a sweet song, and we all felt
honored to hear it.

SUMMER

Once Nate and Matty departed we made our way to Makwa. Distracted by trying to get the best shots possible, we hadn't realized that summer was in full swing. The forest was lush and green. The mosquitoes weren't nearly as bad as they'd been just a week before. As darkness descended on our first night alone, we fell asleep to a whip-poor-will's repetitive song.

In the morning a thin veil of fog floated over the lake as we slid our canoe into the water. The cliffs next to that campsite are always spectacular, but to float under them as the sun's first rays cast a soft glow over the striped rock made rolling out of our sleeping bags at dawn worthwhile. As we drifted below the rock, our necks craned upward, a pair of loons alighted with a chorus of haunting calls. We were on the move.

Our route to Adams Lake that day felt like classic summer adventuring in the Boundary Waters. We portaged to Hoe Lake through thick drooping alders. On our way to Boulder Lake we were each followed by a cloud of circling flies. They dissipated once we emerged from the woods into a breeze coming off the lake. Relieved, we both went for a swim and then ate lunch, basking on a sun-baked rock. We were serenaded with "Oh, sweet Canada Canada Canada"—the song of a white-throated sparrow, and it took us a few minutes to locate its black-and-white-striped head with yellow above its eyes.

The next day we paddled across Adams toward Beaver and Trapline Lakes, and eventually the Kawishiwi River. We stopped for lunch on a clifftop campsite on Malberg Lake and then headed for the Louse River. We paddled past a campsite where folks bustled amidst clothing, gear, and canoes sprawled everywhere, and then we were alone. We snaked our way through a narrows, carefully avoiding rocks.

In the late afternoon we popped out onto Trail Lake and headed for a campsite on a point. Tall grasses growing in the fire grate indicated it was seldom used.

We awoke the next morning to clouds looming overhead and a strong wind from the south that caused the tent to flutter. Traveling would have been foolish, so we shut our eyes again, only to not be able to fall back asleep. After a half hour lying there, we got dressed. As we boiled water for coffee, we noticed a black shape bobbing in the middle of the channel, heading for our campsite. It was too big to be a duck, too round to be a loon, and it had two rounded ears and a snout. It was a bear! Noticing us, the bear frantically swam back

Paddling below the Makwa cliffs

to the shore it had just departed. It climbed out of the water, soggy fur dripping, and scrambled into the underbrush.

We tuned in to WTIP just in time to catch a severe thunderstorm warning issued by the weather service. We could hear concern in the voices of the radio hosts. Just a week before, a storm had hit Duncan Lake and the Height of Land portage with a vengeance, mowing down massive red and white pines as if they were matchsticks and killing Craig Walz, Congressman Tim Walz's brother. With the tragedy striking so close to home, we were cautious.

We managed to drink our first cups of coffee, eat muesli, and button everything up by the time the rain started. The canoe was overturned and tied to a root ball. The tent was reinforced with extra guy-lines. The dishes were washed. The food was packed. We tucked ourselves under the awning of the tent, called Tank, brewed more coffee, and took turns reading chapters from *The Boat Who Wouldn't Float* by Farley Mowat while we waited for the rain to pass. Light at first, it proceeded with intensity, drumming on the tent and creating puddles almost instantly. Then, as quickly as it had begun, it let up.

A few days later we paddled to Polly Lake to meet up with teachers John DiChiara and Ali Rotello and five students from Rauner College Prep, a high school in Chicago. It had become an annual tradition for us to paddle or dogsled for a few days with members of the school's wilderness club. The Boundary Waters has many moods. As we paddled and waded up the Phoebe River, the sun played hide-and-seek with bright billowing clouds. It was warm and wading in the water felt good. As we crossed Knight Lake, however, dark clouds appeared behind us. We began paddling with urgency. We had planned to camp on Phoebe Lake, a couple miles ahead, and reached the nearest campsite just moments before the storm struck. Over the next several hours, we huddled under our tarp and played guessing games, swatted mosquitoes, and cooked up a big pot of macaroni and cheese.

The rain stopped by the time we finished dinner, and the lake was like glass. We loaded the canoes and

First campfire with the wilderness club

paddled across Phoebe to a better campsite as the sun set behind the clouds. The mosquitoes must have heard we were coming, because we were greeted by a buzzing swarm. The situation wasn't easy or fun, but the students and their teachers took it in stride, setting up their tents and crawling in for the night.

Twelve hours later we perched on a large sloping rock at the water's edge. The sun peeked out from behind the clouds, and a breeze sent the bugs fleeing into the woods. As the ambivalent weather gave way to blue skies and sunshine, we began traveling toward Alton Lake. We paused for a late lunch and cliff-jumping session on Beth Lake. We hoped that this day would be the one the students remembered— and that perhaps it would even be a little sweeter thanks to the hardships we'd endured the night before. Often we describe the tranquil times, silence, sunset, and countless beautiful moments encountered in wilderness. But there are blizzards and drenching rains that fill the canoe and leave you soggy, wondering if you will ever see the sun again. Then there are bugs, blisters,

and giant portage packs that send you wobbling down the trail. The wilderness is a wonderful teacher. Often its roughest lessons are the ones that stick with us the longest, helping us well after blisters and mosquito bites have faded.

The students had a valuable gift to offer us as well. By this point our canoe had about five thousand miles under her hull, and the rivets that attach the stern seat had loosened and broken over the last month. In the morning the wilderness club paddled our canoe out to Bill Hansen at Sawbill Canoe Outfitters, and the repaired craft was delivered to our campsite that afternoon by Bill's daughter, Clare Shirley, along with her husband, Dan, and their two-month-old daughter, Kit. Clare's grandparents, Frank and Mary Alice Hansen, started Sawbill Canoe Outfitters sixty years ago, and she and Dan were taking over the family business from her parents, Bill and Cindy Hansen.

Clare explained that Kit was a mellow baby. She had spent her first month of life in a yurt and found the sounds of nature soothing. If Kit cried, all Clare had to do was take her outside, and she'd stop instantly.

Cliff jumping on Beth Lake

SUMMER

ON THE FOURTH of July, clouds rolled in and a tailwind from the southwest blew us along. When we reached the Kelso River, we stopped to visit the dolmen, a boulder suspended above the ground by three smaller rocks. It is a mysterious thing. Some say it was constructed by ancient Vikings, others that it was left behind by a Civilian Conservation Corps crew when a nearby fire tower was built, and still others say that it's a glacial erratic.

By the time we completed the mile-and-a-half-long Lujenida portage, our shoulders ached, our legs burned, and sweat ran down our faces. We swatted away mosquitoes. The sense of relief was sweet as a breeze rippled off Zenith Lake and we dropped our loads. After Tank's pack was off he eagerly lapped up cool water from the lake.

Once we reached our site on Mora Lake, Tank immediately chose a spot to nap in the shade, and we went for a swim to cool off. Despite the threat of rain earlier, the sun prevailed for most of the day. That evening was devoid of both fireworks—they're illegal in the Boundary Waters—and picnics. Or maybe every dinner was a picnic. We ate sitting on a rock covered with lichen and moss, overlooking our corner of the lake. The wind kept the mosquitoes at bay as a Swainson's thrush fluted in the distance.

From Mora we progressed to Knife. Everything was lush and vibrant. We enjoyed seeing our beloved campsite with all the trees leafed out and groups of multiple canoes traversing the length of the clear lake. Several sleek loons gracefully emerged from the depths, spotted fish, and dove again as we paddled across Knife, and we realized that they were likely the same hauntingly beautiful birds we'd seen in late November. They had flown down the Mississippi River to the Gulf of Mexico and spent the winter as seabirds, waiting to return to Knife and raise another generation who would continue this ancient migration. All the while we had been repeating our own primal cycle in the Boundary Waters: moving from lake to lake, pitching our tent, cooking meals, and gathering water.

Calligrapha beetle on lichen-covered rock

Paddling along the Granite River

Knife has remained largely unchanged for hundreds of generations of loons. What a stark contrast it must provide to the roads and refineries, cities and factories, farm fields, locks and dams, lights, and noise that await them outside the Wilderness, a gauntlet of "progress" to navigate. With the end of our year approaching, we would face this outside world ourselves soon enough.

After Knife, we followed the border route to Saganaga. The trip was fast and easy. While carrying the canoe and packs across each portage we remembered the difficulty of trekking here at the tail end of winter. The open expanse of Saganaga was surprisingly calm, so we set a course for the mouth of the Granite River.

We camped on an island with a handful of live jack pines and many more that bore the signs of an old forest fire. The fresh green

Wild blueberries

of thick underbrush was framed by the colorless downed trees. We were walking away from camp, letting the massive trunks dictate our route, when specks of purple-blue scattered within the green caught our eyes. Blueberries! They burst in our mouths with the flavor of summer. Store-bought blueberries may be bigger, but they are tasteless compared to their wild cousins. We picked as many as we could find, eating most but saving a handful for later.

The next day we portaged around Saganaga Falls. The intense rains had swelled the Granite River, allowing us to easily line up several of the rapids, towing our canoe on a rope. The sun was out, and wading in the churning rapids, sometimes up to our waists, was pleasant. Along the way, we passed through rugged bedrock-lined passages and idyllic sun-soaked banks dotted with fruit-laden blueberry bushes. This area had been altered by the big storm. Saw cuts in pines and spruces still released their aroma along several portage trails. A campsite on Clove Lake was closed. This was just the beginning of the devastation we would see.

A short paddle from the portage, we found a campsite perched high above a crumbling granite cliff face. It was unoccupied, and we quickly settled in. After the tent was up, we decided to take advantage of the wind and sunshine by washing most of our clothes and taking a swim. We spent more time than usual writing emails that evening because the United States Forest Service (USFS) was hosting a public listening session in Duluth and we wanted to remind friends and family to attend. Later we would learn that Levi had read a statement Amy prepared—and that the majority of comments made were in favor of protecting the Boundary Waters.

RAIN ROLLED IN after we had clambered into the tent for the night. Lightning flashed and thunder rumbled in the distance.

In the early morning we woke to the sound of a canoe passing below our perch. The air was so still we could hear the bow parting the water. A paddle clunked on the gunwales and the man in the stern told his partner to switch sides. Another thunderstorm arrived about half an hour later. We thought of these unknown paddlers, hoping they were safe and dry.

We made our coffee and ate the last of our granola and powdered milk. That wasn't enough food, so we made the last of our lentil soup, too. Our friends Eric and Jessa Frost were coming to meet us. But looking out at the storm-churned water, we hoped they would make a sound decision when it came time to launch their canoe. We had seen Eric once already, when he came in to write the song with Jerry, but this would be our first time seeing Jessa since the previous September. Eric and Jessa are a wonderful example of how important wilderness is, not just to birds and bugs, plants and the planet, but to people, drawn to live and work in close proximity to it. Eric and Dave grew up a mile away from each other in the suburbs of Chicago, but they met working at Sawbill Canoe Outfitters and eventually founded the Wilderness Classroom together. Eric and Jessa settled in Tofte, Minnesota, a couple hundred yards from Lake Superior and a stone's throw from the Sawbill Trail, which leads north to the Boundary Waters. Like so many other people, they moved here in large part because of the pristine water and wild spaces that are abundant in northeastern Minnesota.

We met Eric, Jessa, and their dog, Otis, near the Wilderness boundary to help carry supplies across the last portage. It was covered in some of the largest wild blueberries any of us had ever seen. Our primal gathering instincts rose from within, and we happily picked berries, visiting as we stuffed ourselves. We filled a container and our bellies, leaving thousands of plump ripe berries for the next fortunate canoeist or black bear. Time was of no consequence. It was a joy to watch Eric and Jessa's stresses, schedules, and deadlines slough off and fade. Like mayflies hatching, we were all transformed by the simple act of gathering food surrounded by the sounds of rushing water, leaves dancing in the breeze, and people we cared about enjoying themselves.

We made the short paddle to our campsite. It felt so good to sit around the fire grate with friends, relaxing and talking as if no time had passed since we last saw each other. It began to rain while we were cooking the new potatoes, green beans, and brats Eric and Jessa had brought, so we hung up a tarp and ate under it. As we sipped tea after dinner, the rain and wind died while dusk descended, resulting in an onslaught of mosquitoes. Suddenly, all four of us were scurrying around to pack up for the night. Jessa remarked that seeing three people who had been to the Amazon so perturbed put the intensity of the bugs in the Boundary Waters into perspective. Relief came only after we retreated to our respective tents and squished all the invaders who had snuck in with us.

We woke up to a few rays of sun making their way through the achromatic clouds. We heard the clinking of Otis's tags and knew he had been kicked out of Eric and Jessa's tent. It didn't take long before his inquisitive furry face was at the tent door, looking for Tank. The sun made its appearance in earnest as we launched our two canoes on the Granite River.

We made quick work of the remaining upstream travel to Magnetic Lake. We lined up the last set of rapids easily and climbed into our canoe at the top. Paddling across Magnetic in a significant west wind gave us a small taste of what we could expect on the more formidable Gunflint Lake.

As our four paddles plied the waves on Magnetic, something had changed: we had just exited the Boundary Waters Canoe Area Wilderness. The 1.1 million acre Wilderness Area is actually made up of three distinct sections: the main body of the Wilderness, where we had traveled and camped for the year so far; the Gunflint Unit, also called the Bruce Vento Unit; and the Trout Lake Unit. The Forest Service recognizes specific travel corridors that people can use to pass between these sections without a new permit. There are a couple ways to pass into the Trout Lake Unit and only one way to officially pass into the Gunflint Unit—through Magnetic, Gunflint, Little Gunflint, and North Lakes, before reentering the Wilderness at South Lake.

We had thought this decision through, discussing it with each other and friends and soliciting opinions from readers of our blog on the Save the Boundary Waters website. Would our experience be altered by canoeing past cabins and resorts? Would others' perceptions of our year change? These were considerations, but we concluded that we wanted to include these different sections. They were parts of the Boundary Waters too. So Dave had called the Gunflint district office to inform the USFS of our crossing, and we were still traveling under our original permit.

On Gunflint, we effectively had a tailwind down the eight-mile length of the lake. If we had been traveling in the opposite direction we would not have made any progress. Instead we flew. The sun was high overhead and we had smiles on our faces. Conversation was kept to a minimum, since our attention was focused on pointing our crafts in the right direction to ride the waves and prevent taking on water or capsizing. Every few miles we ducked behind a point and checked in. The waves were quite big by the time we reached the eastern shore and turned into the narrow passageway to Little Gunflint. We parked the canoes on the sand and ate lunch

Tank rode in the canoe while we waded

SUMMER

while Otis braved the rough water for a swim and Tank napped in the shade.

A motorboat passed us and began fishing where a small rapids pours into Little Gunflint. We commenced lining up the rapids on the opposite side from them. It, too, was quick and easy, and we guessed that most rock hazards must have been removed long ago to help motorboats access good fishing on the expansive North Lake.

North Lake proved to be our biggest challenge of the day, as we had to angle into the wind to reach the Height of Land portage. It was only fair that we would get a taste of the power that had pushed us along for most of the day. It was hard work and we barely made forward progress. Again we entered a period of intense focus, straining our muscles and keeping the canoes pointed in the right direction.

The Height of Land portage looked as if a giant had stomped through and ripped trees from the ground in a fit of rage. Many trees had been cut and pulled to the side of the portage by the Forest Service. As we paddled down South Lake, we looked for a campsite. We had heard that there were three closed sites on the lake and we found all of them. Looking out across the lake, we saw spots that had been mowed down by the wind, leaving swaths of trees broken off twenty feet or so above the ground, standing out in brown patches amid the green of relatively intact forest.

Closer inspection revealed individual tree trunks, standing there naked of green branches, with their tops left in ragged splinters. The site we finally chose was nestled in a bay at the mouth of a stream. The forest was mainly comprised of cedars, some quite large. Only a few had been knocked down, and the tent pads and latrine trail had been cleared. A few cedar and white pine trunks stood at an odd angle to the ground, with half of their root structure elevated. The wind had disrupted these trees, but not toppled them. We wondered if they would survive or if they too would eventually drop, their roots no longer able to hold them in an altered position. After seeing all this destruction we also wondered what it must have sounded like as the wind blew through.

Birch trees mowed down by the wind

THE NEXT MORNING we paddled and portaged to Rose Lake. There is a grandeur to the topography in this part of the Boundary Waters. The hills and cliffs are bigger, with protrusions of bedrock and sheer faces rising up from the earth thanks to the shifting of tectonic plates, the scouring action of glaciers, and the constant carving action of flowing water.

Remarkably, a coveted campsite lined with majestic white pines and a commanding view of the undulating hills was available. So we pitched our tents before paddling over to explore the misty recesses of the waterfall that plummets from Duncan Lake to Rose along the Stairway portage. Down in the groove worn over centuries, we were in a unique world. It was like the rainforest, perpetually humidified by the spray from the cascading water, green and lush with moss. The roar of falling water drowned out all external sounds. We got soaked, but it didn't matter on such a mild summer day.

Exploring Rose Falls

After marveling at the falls and rushing water, we followed the Border Route Trail to an overlook high above Rose and sat silently, feeling the breeze on our faces. We enjoyed the fresh take on both where we had been and prospective routes across the shimmering water below. We hiked the portage to Duncan and thought about the night of the storm. We couldn't bring ourselves to visit the site where Craig Walz had died.

Back in camp, we turned on the satellite phone and received a message from Ellie Siler with the Campaign to Save the Boundary Waters. She wanted to know if we could be back on the Ely side of the Wilderness by Thursday to meet up with Harry Smith from *Sunday TODAY*. Over dinner it sunk in that this was a big deal, though we were somewhat hesitant to change our plans. We had just arrived in the Gunflint Unit and planned to spend a couple weeks exploring this part of the Boundary Waters. To make it back to the appointed spot, we would have to leave the next morning. Reluctantly, we agreed to do it.

After breakfast we parted company with Eric, Jessa, and one of the most idyllic campsites we've ever stayed at. Otis was distraught to see Tank hop in our canoe. Tank, on the other hand, seemed relieved to have some time to recover from chasing Otis.

FROM ROSE LAKE we headed west, retracing our route along the US/ Canada border. We made good progress thanks to light winds and the extended hours of daylight. It was fun to go with the flow on the Granite River, running a couple of the rapids instead of portaging around. We passed quite a few people out enjoying the gorgeous weather, and ate as many blueberries as we could before heading north. A black bear that had been feasting near Devil's Elbow scurried into the woods as it heard us approach.

Saganaga was buzzing with the incremental drone of motorboats. We selected a campsite on an island across from a family with one. They seemed to have somewhere to be every

Overlooking Rose Lake

half hour, firing up their engine and buzzing away only to come back a brief while later. Were we now more sensitive to this loud noise?

Despite our haste, we laid over there for a day due to thunderstorms rolling through. The sky sputtered rain off and on all morning, threatening a downpour, and a substantial wind riled up the lake. In the afternoon the light disappeared, we ran for cover, and the sky let loose. We waited out the deluge, attempting to read aloud for entertainment. We had to give up during the most intense spurts because neither of us could speak loudly enough to be heard over the powerful drumming of raindrops on the tarp.

Tank cowered under the tarp and we calmed him during the loudest bouts of thunder. The earth couldn't absorb the precipitation fast enough, so puddles developed around us. Tank ran for higher ground and the security of low-hanging balsam branches. Then the hail started. Dime-sized white orbs pummeled our overturned canoe, our tarp, and the ground around us with an indiscriminate ferocity. But it didn't last long.

The next day, we camped near the west end of Knife. We were reminded there of what a canoeist's highway the border route still is. From our site, we watched and heard group after group paddling past, some singing, some chatting. One Boy Scout saw Tank and insisted to his friends that he was a wolf. Most groups made a stop at Isle of Pines to see where Dorothy Molter had once sold root beer. Given the hot, sunny weather, we wished she was still there.

We spent the evening listening to news coverage of a second listening session taking place in Ely. The next day marked the close of a thirty-day public input period regarding the USFS and BLM decision about whether or not to renew Twin Metals' two expired mineral leases.

As we headed from Knife to Birch Lake to meet with Harry, the Campaign to Save the Boundary Waters delivered the 74,000 petition signatures that they and their 30 partner organizations had gathered to the USFS office in Duluth. The warm air and water made us confident, so we decided to run or line as many rapids as we could, comfortably navigating through the alternating flat water and shallow rapids. We made it to Birch by lunchtime and settled into a campsite after eating a leisurely meal in the shade of a cedar. The site was near enough to the edge of the Wilderness to pick up a cell signal, so we checked the weather and downloaded our email. It looked as if we were in for a thunderstorm that night. Tracking its progress on the radar, we figured it would hit in the wee hours of the morning. We selected a tent spot among the cedars and firs, tidied camp as best we could, and settled in for the night. Tank opted to sleep under a tree despite the onslaught of mosquitoes at dusk.

Around three o'clock in the morning, we woke with a start as wind buffeted the tent and lightning strobed. How could our tent be shuddering and flapping so much? It was in the forest, sheltered from every direction. Dave shot up and unzipped the door, explaining that he was going to check on the canoe. He didn't bother to put on any clothes, just stepped into his sandals and ran toward the lake.

The sickening crack of tree trunks breaking caused us both to operate without thinking and dart for the shoreline, along with Tank. We were instantly soaked by the gusting rain. The rapid-fire lightning prevented us from going out to a nearby point, so we stood in the northwest corner of the campsite, downwind of just one tall pine and a spruce swaying in the erratic wind. We huddled there, keeping our eyes trained on the two trees, ready to run if part or all of them started to topple.

We donned our raingear, oblivious to having been cold until we stopped shivering. Every once in a while we saw a distinct bolt of lightning in the distance. Tank seemed most perturbed by the riled-up lake, barking and biting at the waves before we called him back. About then a wave of emotion hit us. Up until that point, there had been no time to register fear or think about how easily we could have died. Trees and branches had fallen around us before either of us had reached a safe spot. Now that the danger had passed, we realized how lucky we were. It was one of the most dangerous situations we had experienced in all of our wilderness travels.

As the wind mellowed, we assessed the damage. Two other campsites were in sight of ours, across the water, and we hoped that if anyone in those parties was in trouble they would be out signaling with a light. We weren't venturing across the roiling lake unless we saw obvious signs of distress. Our canoe was unharmed

but entangled in the limbs of a large cedar that had snapped four feet off the ground. The trunk now rested at an angle, suspended inches above the gunwales. Several spruces and balsam firs had been similarly snapped and blown several feet from their jagged stumps. Most alarmingly, a thick branch had broken off a tall ash and fallen about twenty feet, just short of the tent.

The next morning, after a couple fitful hours of sleep, the pulse of a motor interrupted the usual birdsong while we were making coffee. A helicopter circled and then hovered above the treetops to the northwest. It looked like it was a lake or two over—Basswood? The drone of the Forest Service floatplane also entered our soundscape, and we watched it swoop low, making a couple passes before dipping out of sight behind distant trees. A sinking feeling developed in the pits of our stomachs. This kind of activity in the Boundary Waters could only mean one of two things—a serious injury or death.

We paddled to four nearby sites to check on their occupants. Everyone had come out a little shaken but unharmed. They were all drying

We were lucky our canoe wasn't crushed

wet sleeping bags and clothing in the sun. One group had a tent pole break in the wind. Another had a tree fall just feet from a tent. It was a relief to know that everyone nearby was OK. Later that day, however, we would hear the explanation for the helicopter and plane: two people in a Boy Scout group had died on the Quetico side of Basswood Lake. A white pine had fallen on their tent. The sadness we felt for all involved was amplified by having experienced the storm ourselves. This outcome was entirely based on chance—that they had chosen that campsite and that particular place to pitch a tent, that the initial blast of wind had pummeled and overtaken a nearby tree. It could have been us. Nature has a way of revealing our fragility and lack of control.

A group of friends—Becky Rom, Paul Schurke, and Nancy Piragis— were slated to come in with Harry Smith. They were all delayed. Outside the Boundary Waters, trees blocked driveways and roads. The power was out in town. Paul happened to be lodging a crew of painters at Wintergreen. Wielding chainsaws, they set to work cutting trees until

SUMMER

the five-mile stretch of gravel road to the Kawishiwi Trail was cleared.

We met everyone as they unloaded canoes and gear from a motorboat that had shuttled them to the portage into Birch Lake. Then we escorted them to our campsite. Harry had gone on a trip here when he was in high school, and it was clear that he was happy to be back. Although he was only with us for a couple hours, he checked off key items on the Boundary Waters bucket list: he filled his bottle and drank right from the lake, went swimming from our campsite, and got bit by deerflies. By the end of their time with us, Harry's face revealed just how much being in the wilderness had allowed him to recharge. And as they paddled away we wished they could have stayed a little longer.

×

WE MADE OUR way back to Knife for a few days. The groups we encountered on the portage trails still seemed shaken by the storm, exchanging knowing looks with us.

The sun was intense, the air still, and we were drenched in sweat by the time we reached our campsite. A swim in Knife's clear deep water was in order. That evening we watched two loons fishing off the point. A bald eagle swooped down and plucked a fish from the water, barely disturbing its mirrorlike surface.

One day two canoes paddled by Girl Scouts arrived with a resupply, singing "We're off to find the Freemans" to the melody of "We're Off to See the Wizard." We enjoyed several hours with them, going over a map together and talking about the places we had visited over the course of what was now more than three hundred days in the Wilderness, showing them the proposed Twin Metals mine site and explaining where the water flows. Maybe someday those girls will follow the water even further, all the way to the Arctic Ocean. You never know where skills honed and dreams planted in the Boundary Waters might take you.

Next, we traveled to Basswood in what felt like the peak of summer. The days were long, the sun was intense, and fair-weather clouds scattered across blue skies reflected off the lake's surface, which was plied by

Burying Jacob and Jonah in the sand

the occasional canoe. The singsongy voice of a white-throated sparrow rang through the forest. One evening, at our site on Pipestone Bay, the golden hour descended and the dark silhouettes of dragonflies maneuvered above us with the low-angle light glinting off their wings. Mosquitoes were still present, but none bit us because they had met their match in this darting predator.

Later we headed toward US Point and found a campsite known as "the Hilton" vacant. Jason and the Goldsteins were coming in, and this time Joseph, now fifteen, was bringing his whole family: his mother, Kemia, his dad, Jeff, and his three brothers, Jacob (12), Joshua (6), and Jonah (6). As we spotted three canoes approaching, our world suddenly took on the frenetic pace of four boys out for adventure. We fished, we swam, we buried each other in sand on the beach.

The next day was spent fishing just a couple miles from our campsite. We dropped our anchors (mesh bags we had filled with rocks) on a reef in twenty feet of water. Our three canoes floated close enough that we could carry on a conversation. It wasn't long before a feisty walleye found Joseph's lure, and shortly after he had it in the boat, Jacob worked to land a 20-inch smallmouth bass. Kemia and Jeff assisted the Littles—Joshua and Jonah—sticking bait on their hooks and helping them each reel in a fish. Joshua was so excited as his dad lifted his first smallmouth out of the water we thought he was going to leap right out of the canoe. For several hours it seemed like at least one person was battling a fish, and doubles were not uncommon. We released most of the fish immediately, keeping only what we would eat for dinner.

Back on land, Joseph set up a fish-filleting station and proceeded to instruct his younger brothers, deftly filleting one fish before handing the knife to Jacob. Joseph offered words of encouragement and advice as Jacob made the first few tentative cuts. The younger boys sat, mesmerized by the actions of their big brothers.

We traveled with this lively crew to a spot on the Basswood River, then parted ways all too soon. We enjoyed seeing how this family operated—so tightly bonded, yet each member exuding their own personality and creativity. We drew strength from the boundless energy of the boys, and from the entire family's love of this place.

We paddled to Crooked Lake and set up camp in a sprawling campsite on Thursday Bay. We were enveloped in a gray fog and the shoreline across the way disappeared, but the golden ruffled heads of chanterelle mushrooms starred the forest floor. The next day we headed to Friday Bay and unloaded the canoe in a campsite with a pink rock slab angling down to the water.

Later that evening, a gentle breeze blew past our expansive granite shore. The sun was getting low in the sky and a legitimate chill was in the air. This was the first evening in a long while that we felt pleasantly cool before going to bed. We enjoyed it so much that we hesitated before adding another layer of clothing.

AS WE PADDLED along the Nina Moose River, the water cut a dark channel through swaying green stalks of wild rice that rose nearly to the tops of our heads. Wild rice is the abundant and entirely water-dependent food source of this area, sacred to the Anishinaabe and linked to their ancestral history. Many generations ago they traveled here from the eastern United States, following instructions of a vision to move toward the setting sun until they came to the place where there is food on the water.

We had paddled through wild rice beds countless times, but this was the first time we were able to isolate the scent, rich and grain-like. Our senses had become more sensitive over the course of the year. We had smelled algae on some lakes and could differentiate between the scents of cedar and pine. The perfumy smell of Labrador tea alerted us to the presence of a bog long before we caught sight of it. We'd recognized the barnyard smell of moose and the musky scent of beaver. We could even smell the other canoeists we passed on portages or the water, carrying the aromas of soap, sunscreen, bug spray, and sometimes cigarettes.

Wild rice along the Nina Moose River

How would this heightened sense of smell serve us back in a city, where we'd be accosted by the scents of car exhaust, gasoline, urine, and perfume? In a wild place one's sense of smell serves a purpose, providing subtle cues about one's surroundings and the creatures in it.

THE SOUND OF something substantial cutting through the air directly overhead caught our attention. Two gleaming white trumpeter swans landed amid the green stalks of wild rice and began grabbing them with their black bills. Their long necks curved as they gobbled up the rice. Over and over, they repeated the process with practiced bobs of their heads. Trumpeter swans were hunted to near extinction, but now they are coming back. Each year a few more can be seen in the Boundary Waters. Due to its sensitivity to water pollution, wild rice is this region's canary in the coal mine. Sulfate, like that which could result downstream of Twin Metals, turns into sulfide in the mucky bottom of lakes and streams. Sulfide

Trumpeter swans landing

is toxic to wild rice. If copper mines are built upstream of the Boundary Waters, wild rice will be one of the first plants to suffer. What would this do to animals like the swans?

On Nina Moose Lake we would meet up with Becky Rom, her husband, Reid Carron, and Daniel Slager, publisher and CEO of Milkweed Editions. We had been in touch with Daniel since February, after soliciting our friends for advice and connections to help us potentially produce a book. We knew that if we began the process of thinking about a book after we exited, it would be too late for it to serve as a tool to protect the Boundary Waters from the mining threat. Daniel had read samplings of our blog posts, social media, and journals, and had decided to paddle into the Wilderness to meet a couple potential authors, apparently a first for him. And so over sandwiches and fresh fruit supplied by Becky and Reid, we got to know Daniel, learned more about Milkweed—which we already knew had published some of our favorite books, including Karsten Heuer's *Being Caribou* and Seth Kantner's *Ordinary Wolves*— and found out what it would take to

write one ourselves. Our conversation continued from the campsite to the canoes as we escorted our visitors toward the entry point.

Our world grew quiet as we paddled back to camp alone. The scent of the wild rice enveloped us once more, and the swoosh of swan wings was the only sound. Their huge bodies made disproportionately small splashes as they landed on the glassy water in front of our camp. The swans, the rice they were eating, the pure water that rice grows in, and the potential for people in the distant future to experience it all—this renewed our motivation. We had reached thousands of people through photos and text posted online, but a book would allow us to reach even more. It would be a chance for us to tell our story— and the story of the Wilderness.

LEAVING THE WILD rice and the swans behind, we made our way west to Ge-be-on-e-quet Lake and then to Eugene Lake. Along the way we paddled past a loon family. Two adult loons with their two young ones were

Wild rice, not quite ripe yet

on a fishing venture, drifting in the waves, peering down into the water and diving. The young ones were getting big. Their plumage even resembled that of an adult, with white bellies and dark brown heads and backs. Not long ago they had been little balls of fluff, riding on their parents' backs.

The western part of the Boundary Waters was new to us. We had paddled and dogsledded through Lac La Croix several times, but never explored the small lakes to the south. Fires in this area in the 1860s left sparser patches of virgin forest and fire-scarred trees, so these less desirable trees were spared from logging. In contrast to parts of the forest that had been logged, like the shores of Basswood or Knife, here the occasional massive white pine towered above the rest of the forest. Portaging past these giants was unreal. We couldn't help but reach out to touch their deeply furrowed bark. How old were they? What had they seen, what storms and fires had they lived through? One of the behemoths had fallen, its roots sticking two stories into the air above a basement-sized hole left in the ground. What would it have felt like to be in the presence of this tree when it fell?

Amy admires one of the giant white pines

We lingered among the towering pines as long as we could, but the wild rice was ripening and would wait for no one. We worked our way back to Nina Moose Lake to meet our friends Bert and Johnnie Hyde, and Lynden and Lawson Gerdes, who would join us for a few days and teach us how to harvest the bounty. The two couples had built cabins in the woods long ago and still live close to the land, growing food and gathering water, berries, and rice.

Tick, tick, tick, tick: the sound of wild rice kernels landing in our canoe signaled we were in a good spot. We paddled and pushed the canoe through the thick stalks, which narrowed our field of vision to the green and golden plants in front of us and the patch of blue sky directly above. We fell into a rhythm, one person maneuvering the canoe while the other carefully bent the stalks over the boat with one cedar flail and lightly stroked it with the other.

In the afternoon we carefully scooped handfuls of rice into one of our packs for the trip back to our campsite. Then we spread the rice out on tarps to dry in the sun and sifted through the kernels, hunting

Harvesting wild rice

SUMMER

for small white caterpillars that were feasting on the rice, leaving empty hulls in their wake. As we did this, we observed an ant crawling through the rice. It headed straight for a caterpillar and latched on with its pincers! About five times the size of the ant, the caterpillar writhed around like a bronco attempting to buck a cowboy off its back. But a couple other ants joined in, and soon the caterpillar was being dragged down into the ants' lair. We looked more closely and saw that all over the pile of wild rice, little insect dramas were unfolding as the ants hunted the caterpillars.

We had picked our fair share of berries and fried up plenty of fish, but we had never gathered food in such a deliberate and steady manner. What a wonderful gift these lakes and streams had provided. We hadn't tasted a single grain of the rice yet, but we felt nourished in ways that a trip to the grocery store could never yield.

After two days spent paddling and pushing the canoe through thick beds of wild rice combined with constantly lifting and moving the flails, sore muscles inspired us to stop early and soak in the cool tumbling rapids overlooking the same bed of rice we had worked so hard in. Cool water bubbled and swirled around our tired limbs as we watched Bert guide a canoe through the rice, expertly adjusting its speed to match Johnnie's flails. A few yards away, Lynden and Lawson snaked their own path. They made it look so effortless and graceful, dancing through the rice.

They taught us a lot during their brief stay: how to harvest rice, hang tarps, use a crooked knife, and identify plants. Most importantly, they taught us that although we had learned a lot during our year, we had just skimmed the surface. There are many lifetimes' worth of knowledge hidden in the wilderness. If we listen, learn, and practice, perhaps someday we too could dance effortlessly through the rice. Perhaps happiness doesn't require piles of money, but living with purpose. Relaxing in that pool with a pack full of rice waiting at the end of the portage filled us with another kind of wealth.

Our time harvesting wild rice renewed our conviction to keep these waters clean so that the Anishinaabe, the swans, and others might do the same next fall, and for many years to come. Future generations deserve the chance to float among the head-high stalks and breathe in the same aroma we did—to winnow the rice, parch it, taste it, and be nourished by it.

WITH ONLY TWO weeks left in the wilderness, there was still much to see and do. The inevitable reality of concluding our year in the Boundary Waters was beginning to fill us with apprehension. As we started to travel back to the Kawishiwi River, where our adventure had begun, we slowed down. On Agnes Lake we pitched our tent on a carpet of red pine needles, sheltered by the trees' branches. Sitting on a rock and watching the sun dance off the waves, we tried to etch the sights, sounds, and smells around us into our brains. The transition into fall weather gradually snuck up on us. The nights were cooler—perfect weather to be nestled into a sleeping bag.

After reluctantly crawling out of our warm cocoons one morning, we noticed that Tank was keenly interested in the crooked branches above the fire grate. An agitated pine marten peered down at us. It shifted its hold on the branch and growled at Tank. How had it got up there without us noticing? We secured Tank to a tree on the opposite side of the

The pine marten waited for us to leave

SUMMER

campsite, but the marten remained on its perch, waiting for us to pack up and leave.

We paddled and portaged to Stuart Lake, then set up camp under fledgling red pines. The next day we headed out to the Stuart River after a leisurely morning, cinching our hoods against a light misty rain. Wild rice was growing in the shallow water of Whitefeather Lake, and we wished we still had our flails. The bog plants were starting to turn color, the burnt tinge to the leatherleaf providing a contrast to golden-tan grasses. Several pileated woodpeckers were apparently unfazed by the rain, their drumbeat reverberating into the forest. Canada geese were congregating for their migration south, and a flock flew low past us. Although the birds were preparing for the winter, we were not yet ready to leave.

Rainy weather followed us through Crooked Lake and up the Basswood River. Thick cloud cover, cool temperatures, and a steady rain seemed to characterize fall in the Boundary Waters. The first frost warning of the season was issued, and we cinched our sleeping bags tight for the first time in months. In the morning the cold tips of our noses suggested that the temperature had dropped below freezing. Blades of grass glistened in the morning light for a fleeting moment before thawing. Fog ebbed and flowed across the smooth black water and we sat in silence, not wanting the snap of a twig or the clank of a pot to break the spell.

There is a primal enchantment aroused when you wake to a blanket of mist covering your temporary home deep in the Boundary Waters. We often find ourselves fiddling with dials and switches, trying in vain to capture the moment with our cameras, but on this morning we just soaked in the light, mist, water, and silence.

Maybe it's best that the camera can't capture the cool moist air soothing trail-worn muscles or the sound of swans skimming the treetops and disappearing into the fog. Moments like these fuel our souls and bring into focus the intangible values of the wilderness.

This is the real world—wild, free, and untrammeled. We don't find it on our phones, computer screens, televisions, or radios, no matter

Misty morning light

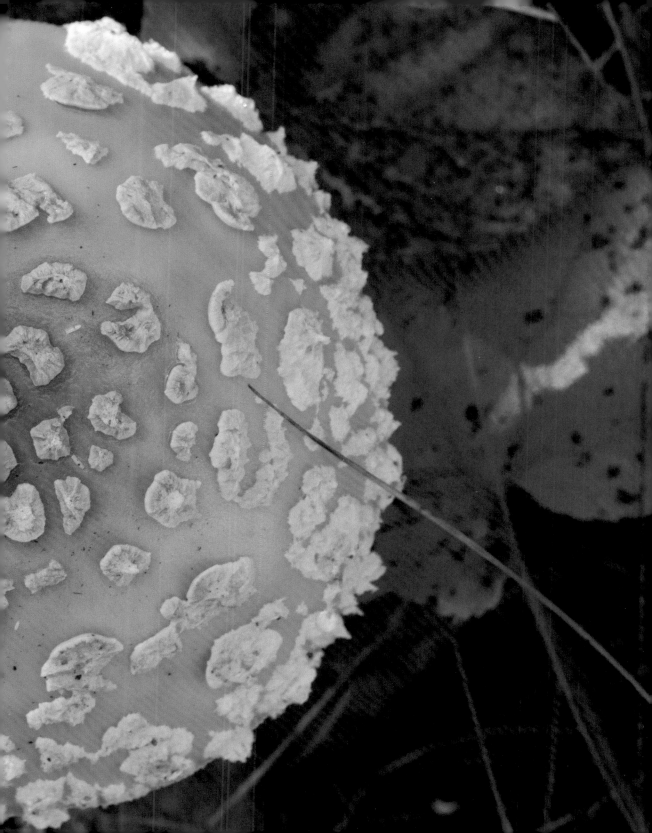

how many times we surf the web or change the channel. We have to put all that noise away and make pilgrimages to wild places; we have to slow down, unplug, and just be. Photos and videos can't fully capture these moments, but hopefully our words and images can provide a taste to the uninitiated and a welcome reminder to seasoned wilderness travelers of the wonders their public lands hold.

✕

WE APPROACHED THE mile-long portage around Basswood Falls and greeted a man coming the other way with an aluminum canoe on his shoulders. He asked if we were Dave and Amy as he plopped the canoe in the water, and explained that his instructor from the Voyageur Outward Bound School (VOBS) had told him about us. His instructor and several other students soon came along. We chatted a little and then headed across the portage, carrying half our load.

When we got to the other end of the portage a booming voice said, "Hi Dave and Amy!" It was Steve Johnson, a legendary canoe guide who has seen many more Boundary Waters sunsets than we had over the course of a full year there. We eventually began our trek back down the trail to get the rest of our gear, but didn't get far before we ran into the VOBS group carrying our barrels. They didn't have anything else to pick up, so they had just decided to do something nice for us! They thanked us for our efforts to protect the Boundary Waters and we invited them to the "exit party," now only a week away. As we paddled off we noted what a rare and special pleasure it was to know someone at both ends of a portage.

Sitting in our tent on Newfound several days later, we tried to distill our thoughts and feelings into one final blog post for the Campaign to Save the Boundary Waters. We tried to describe what the Boundary Waters had taught us and how we were bracing ourselves for the shock of being back in civilization, but we had trouble putting such strong feelings into words. More than anything, we realized we were more nervous about leaving the Wilderness than we had been about entering it

Launching our canoe on the Basswood River

SUMMER

a year ago. Perhaps John Muir said it best: "Going to the woods is going home."

That evening the lake was transformed into perfect stillness. Clouds had rolled in, and lightning illuminated the western end from time to time. Although the sunset itself had been undramatic, the lightning bursts were orange and pink, illuminating a dark purple blanket of clouds. A single wolf howled in the distance.

After a couple hours of tossing and turning we climbed out of the tent and walked to the lake in hopes of catching a glimpse of the harvest moon. The white orb above the birches and firs was so bright that we didn't need our headlamps. Faint rustlings coming from multiple directions indicated that the forest was bustling with activity. A flying squirrel chattered and scrambled up a birch trunk. The wolf howled again. Loons sounded an alarmed yodeling call. We crawled back into our sleeping bags, willing ourselves to feel tired only to have a northern saw-whet owl begin its constant "toot, toot, toot, toot." Sleep would have to wait.

Trumpeter swans at dawn

THE "OH, SWEET Canada Canada Canada" song of a white-throated sparrow surprised us as we portaged into Thomas, conjuring memories of summer. We hadn't heard this song in quite a while, which led us to assume that these birds had all flown south. And apparently they all had except this one, because we heard no more in our remaining days. The wind was significant the next day. We were glad that it was a tailwind for most of the way—and to be off the water before it reached its peak. We set up camp early, near where the Kawishiwi River enters Insula Lake, so we could wash our clothes. We didn't feel dirty or stinky, but figured we had become accustomed to a different standard of cleanliness. The wind dried everything quickly, and we neatly stowed the laundered pants and shirts for our last day in the Boundary Waters.

Lake One was shrouded in fog when we woke two days later. We watched it burn off as we ate breakfast and the sun rose above the trees. A faint squeaky noise came

from the water behind us. An adult loon was fishing with a young one just twenty feet from shore. They slowly worked their way to the southwest, which called our attention to a foreign smell wafting on the breeze. Exhaust fumes. Were we really close enough to the edge of the Wilderness to smell the pollution originating outside it?

We had paddled up the South Kawishiwi River a year ago to bear witness through every season. Now we found ourselves on the South Kawishiwi once again, pitching camp for the last time. That evening, we heard an unusual grunting echoing out over the water. Uncertain of the source, we sat up to listen. It was a moose in rut—another sure sign of fall from an animal attuned to the Earth's rhythms. The Boundary Waters was largely the same as it had been a year ago: changing leaves, crisp and foggy fall mornings, the loons' elegant summer plumage fading. But for us the year had been transformative.

Our final full day in camp was warm and sunny. Tank slept in the sun, only getting up to choose a new spot as the light shifted. We used the time to gather our thoughts, prepare

Dewdrops on spotted jewelweed

SUMMER

our speeches, and hatch last-minute plans for the following day.

Black-capped chickadees moved through the red pines in waves of sound and activity. There was no sign of the moose in rut. We were pretty sure there had been two, due to some rustling in the underbrush and a bit of a call and response. Based on the sounds, we guessed that the bull had been rebuffed.

That night we lay awake, a thin layer of nylon separating us from the world beyond. A year earlier we'd figured we would be excited about sleeping in a bed again, but a hollow feeling filled us instead. The words we had prepared rolled through our minds. The thought of leaving weighed heavily on our hearts. This was the most glorious time of the year in the Boundary Waters, and we had everything we needed: food, water, shelter, companionship.

But our collected voices have the power to effect change, and in many ways our journey was just beginning. We needed to embrace everything we had felt and learned, distill it down to its very essence, and continue to advocate and share it with others. In order to protect

Day 366: Loading our canoe on the last morning

SUMMER

the Wilderness we loved so much, we had to leave it.

×

ON THE MORNING of September 23, we packed up camp for the last time and loaded the canoe. As we made our way to the portage leading out, we savored each paddle stroke and the calm. As soon as we pulled the canoe from the water, we spotted three friends heading our way to document the exit, the first of many people we would meet over the course of the day. Clearly the silence was over.

The portage trail crossed the Wilderness boundary. Somewhere in the middle of it we decided that we should each take an extra-large step to signify our exit from the wilderness and entrance into civilization. In the middle of this nondescript portage there was no sign. There was no change in the character of the forest. The moose and red squirrels hadn't been told where the federally designated Wilderness Area begins or ends.

The water also knows no boundary. The water that we set the canoe in on the other side of the portage was out of the Wilderness. The border encircling the BWCA Wilderness is an imaginary line—a line drawn on a map. In this unfortunate instance the water flows *out* of the wilderness and eventually back *in*. How would this water change if in its time out of the Wilderness it flowed past an industrial mining zone and over a tunnel designed to transport a slurry of toxic waste rock? How would the character of our nation's most popular wilderness area change if it was located downstream of our nation's most toxic industry?

The current pushed us down the course of the river. A howl erupted in the forest to our left and we knew the sled dogs in the Voyageur Outward Bound School's kennel had heard our approach. On our last portage we met more well-wishers and realized this was the first time in an entire year that we'd been in a group of more than nine people. They carried our packs and we only had to make one trip across the portage, squishing through mud and stepping over roots, deeply inhaling the scent of spruce. Passing the Voyageur Outward Bound School, the trickle of people and boats increased to a steady flow.

The Highway 1 bridge came into sight and then two pontoon boats and a couple smaller fishing boats

We were engulfed by the flotilla

approached us. Our heart rates went up and Tank began to whine and wiggle in his seat. Television cameras were mounted on each of the pontoon boats. A reporter skipped the formalities and told his driver that he wanted to get a microphone on one of us. Anxiety and gasoline fumes washed over us as the massive boat approached.

Microphones on, we conducted a surreal interview, paddling as they kept pace with us, peppering us with questions. How could we articulate what we were feeling while bombarded by such an assault to the senses?

As canoes became visible under the bridge, we couldn't help but gasp at the sheer number of people. The steady flow had turned into a flood. Seventy boats converged on us. We paddled into the middle of them and stopped to greet familiar faces. Here were the people who had helped us

SUMMER

countless times and had dedicated so much energy in innumerable ways to protecting this place we all love.

As the water flowed under the hulls of our boats a chant of "speech, speech" arose. Overcome, we choked back tears.

We thanked everyone for being there, acknowledging they were there because of this place by gesturing to the clear sky above, to the woods, and to the water. We scooped it up in our hands and let it fall through our fingers. Its coolness on our palms grounded us and we found the words we had been grasping for. Taking turns, we articulated that we had gone into the Wilderness to bear witness and it had indeed spoken to us.

"The land and water speaks through the call of a loon echoing across a still lake, the muffled fall of snowflakes, the metamorphosis

SUMMER

of dozens of dragonflies, and the smell of wild rice. However, our interpretation of what it said is irrelevant.

What is important is that the land speaks to anyone who takes the time to listen—and so it is imperative that we preserve the BWCAW and all remaining wild land so that future generations have the opportunity to hear it, too. We hope that you continue to take the time to listen—and heed the call to speak loudly in its defense.

We are reentering what some have called "the real world." But we need to set the record straight on this concept. It is the other way around. We are reentering a civilized world, a fast-paced world filled with cars, cell phones, airplanes, and indoor plumbing. But don't for one second think that this is what's real. When we exited the Wilderness, we left the real world—the world where Mother Nature rules, where wolf packs roam freely, where wild rice grows, where mosquitoes hatch, where loon chicks ride on their parents' backs, where the sun rises and sets over forest and lakes that are untrammeled—where no sign of this civilized world exists."

Later we would slowly paddle on toward River Point Resort, talking to friends and acquaintances, hesitant to land. Questions would be asked and photos would be taken. Food would be eaten. Music would be played by our dear friends. The evening, in short, would be a blur in our memory, as we were bombarded by friends, family, well-wishers, and a general sense of happiness and positive energy.

But our thoughts would remain with our footfalls on that last portage. Balancing on the dark rocks at the start, leaving temporary impressions in the mud, they joined those of countless other people, moose, wolves, fox and snowshoe hare that have skirted these rapids. Sunlight filtered through the spruce branches. A raven's coarse call relayed a message through the forest canopy. The river hummed while tumbling over rocky obstacles, perpetually flowing. Under its dark surface lies so much life. The water would continue to flow long after we had left. The seasons would change. Soon ice would encrust the banks and snow would dust the conifers. Its volume would increase in the spring and walleye would come here to spawn as they have for millennia.

ONWARD

The night after exiting the Boundary Waters, we found ourselves enclosed by four walls, lying in a bed, staring at the ceiling. How could anyone sleep like this? The hum of a dehumidifier—what one typically thinks of as innocuous white noise—was jarring and foreign, and it set us on edge. Not able to hear the wind, we worried about the canoe we had left on the beach. Only after securing the canoe and opening the window, letting in a gentle breeze and the sound of rustling leaves, did we finally drift off to sleep.

Within seventy-two hours we had boarded an airplane bound for Washington, DC, to advocate for the Boundary Waters in a different way, meeting face to face with our elected officials. Moving through the air at five hundred miles per hour was mind-boggling in comparison to the pace we had become accustomed to in our canoe.

Many trips by car and plane followed over the next six months. We gave dozens of presentations in seven states. Almost every time someone asked, "What's it like to be back in society?" Or, "How are you adjusting?" Our typical answer—"It's been kind of tough, but we're used to it now"—doesn't begin to address how challenging the readjustment had been for us. We took to calling it recompression, because it is the polar opposite of decompression—what most people experience when they visit the Boundary Waters. As we recompressed we were affected in ways we hadn't anticipated. The biggest challenge, as on that first night, was getting used to falling asleep inside. Our internal clocks were confused by artificial light, and our bodies had adapted to the routine of the trail, our senses so attuned to the woods that sleeping indoors felt unnatural. It took several weeks for us to grow accustomed to being cut off from the sounds of wind rustling in the trees and water lapping against the shore—and no longer smelling freshly fallen pine needles in the duff or the onset of rain.

We were occasionally taken aback by the absurdity of this world of cars, fluorescent lights, and concrete. Turning on a faucet to get a drink of water, we wondered where it came from, the filtration system and the network of pipes it had traveled through to fill our glass, as we remembered simply dipping water bottles over the side of our canoe. In grocery stores we were intimidated by the seemingly endless possibilities for what we could purchase and prepare for dinner. And we found ourselves taking breaks outside crowded rooms. We would prepare ourselves for presentations and events, and balanced those commitments with

time spent going for a walk or a run whenever possible.

Just the thought of returning to the wilderness creates a wave of relief, though. Like two-month-old Kit Shirley, humans are hardwired to be in nature. As one takes a walk in the woods or goes on a weekend camping trip, the blood pressure drops, the prefrontal cortex settles down, and cortisol levels drop. Even a memory from the year we spent in the Boundary Waters can lower our heart rates. The scent of wet earth reminds us of what is important. Fox tracks in the snow or the sound of chickadees grounds us. A run on a wooded trail or watching rain drip through pine branches outside our window allows for a brief escape.

We bore witness to the Boundary Waters Canoe Area Wilderness in every season and came away with a better understanding of its inner workings. Whether one cares to admit it or not, we are tied to the land and dependent on it for our survival. The fight over conservation will continue between those who understand this concept and those who only see land for the commercial value of the resources it contains.

Our year in the Wilderness heightened our senses and pushed us to slow down, live in the moment, and see how precious the wild oases that remain on earth are to humanity and all life. It has become painfully clear that in an age when humans are more disconnected from nature than ever, the future of our species and the eco-systems that support us will be endangered if wilderness is lost. Wilderness is the earth's DNA unaltered, a window into the complex framework of air, water, climate, soil, and nutrients that sustain all life. Wilderness nourishes our souls and is the North Star guiding us toward a sustainable future. We must not lose sight of its value, and we must speak loudly for these quiet places.

AS WEEKS AND months passed we reverted back to our "normal" life on the edge of the Boundary Waters. We rented a small house at the edge of Ely and led dogsledding trips over the following winter. Every week we hoped that the Forest Service and the BLM would announce their decision about Twin Metals' mineral leases. As time passed we grew more anxious. Years of hard work and the fate of the Boundary Waters rested on this decision, and the waiting was unbearable.

On a cold December day the phone rang. It was Becky Rom and she wanted to talk to both of us. As we listened over speakerphone, she told us that the Forest Service and the BLM had just denied the Twin Metals leases—and announced a two-year moratorium on any mining-related activity on federal land within the Boundary Waters watershed, allowing for a comprehensive scientific review of the watershed to determine whether it is the wrong place for sulfide-ore copper mining. The Forest Service also recommended that, for a period of twenty years, there be no new federal mineral leases or federal mineral exploration permits on federal lands within the watershed. The scientific data and public input gathered during the two-year moratorium would inform the Secretary of the Interior's decision on whether the twenty-year withdrawal would actually be enacted.

Smiling and crying, we hugged. A huge weight fell from our chests. We knew the fight to permanently protect the Boundary Waters was far from over, but we also knew that this was a very big step. As we opened our laptops, press releases and emails started pouring in. We spent the rest of the day reaching out to others with the exciting news.

That night, over a bottle of wine, we talked about the path that had led us from Paddling to DC to A Year in the Wilderness, and about all the wonderful people we'd met who are working tirelessly to protect the Boundary Waters. We are powerful when we work together toward a common goal. Back in the summer of 2013, the Campaign to Save the Boundary Waters was an idea supported by a handful of dedicated locals like Becky Rom. Three and a half years later, the Campaign and its partner organizations represent more than 18 million people. Conservation groups, sportsmen, veterans, and faith organizations—people from all across the country—are standing together to protect the Boundary Waters. On that cold winter night, as we read the BLM's announcement aloud a fifth time, it was clear that our collective voice had been heard.

We are more confident than ever that together we will permanently protect the Wilderness from sulfide-ore copper mining, but the road ahead will not be easy. A few days after the government announced the denial of the

mineral leases we invited Becky over for coffee to discuss the path forward. She explained that although things were going well we could not rest on our laurels. The growth the movement had seen over the last three years would have to continue. Major public lands battles often last for a decade or more and the Campaign to Save the Boundary Waters would have to double in size over the next couple years.

Sipping our coffee in silence for a moment, we mulled over the work ahead. In many ways time in the wilderness prepares us for the fights to protect our public lands. At times we are pushed along by a tailwind, with the sun warming the backs of our necks. Minutes later we are slogging across a steep muddy portage, swatting mosquitoes and willing the next lake to appear. There will be victories and headwinds, but the key is to keep moving forward, and to never lose sight of the goal.

One obvious question remained. "So what can we do?" we asked. Becky smiled and said, "Just keep doing what you have been doing. Keep elevating the Wilderness—and finish your book!"

THE BOUNDARY WATERS is a national treasure, like Yellowstone or the Grand Canyon. These lakes, rivers, and forests belong to all of us. And we must all work to ensure that they remain protected for future generations. We hope that you will join us in protecting our nation's most popular wilderness and that you will use this book as a tool to share our story and the Boundary Waters with your community, so that they will become defenders as well.

Visit www.SavetheBoundaryWaters.org to learn more and to take action. Watch *Bear Witness*, the award-winning short film about our year, share it with your friends, and help spread the word. Do you know a business, organization, school, or club that might be interested in hosting a book signing, film screening, or presentation in your area?

We are always looking for avenues to share our story, so please get in touch and connect with us at www.FreemanExplore.com.

The latest threat to the Boundary Waters is potential copper mining within its watershed, but there are countless threats to wild places all over the world. We hope that this book has given you a nudge to stand up for the places you love. It doesn't take a year to fall in love with a place—sometimes all it takes is one sunset, a hike, a brief encounter with wildlife, a clear view of the Milky Way, or even a photograph. This year in the Wilderness heightened our respect for the Boundary Waters and strengthened our resolve to keep it as it is—untrammeled, unpolluted, and wild. Please join us in speaking loudly for quiet places.

ACKNOWLEDGMENTS

It is hard to put into words how grateful we are for the support we have received from so many individuals, organizations, and businesses that made *A Year in the Wilderness* possible. Our biggest concern when we headed into the Boundary Waters was that people would forget about us and our calls to action would go unheard. In retrospect we had nothing to worry about because thousands of people had our backs. You signed petitions; called your elected officials; donated time, money, food, and equipment; delivered supplies; and helped us every step of the way. To everyone who has taken action to help protect the Wilderness: we are humbled and inspired by your generosity, and hope this book will help you continue to speak loudly for this quiet place.

A Year in the Wilderness never would have happened without the leadership of Becky Rom, the hard work of the Northeastern Minnesotans for Wilderness board, and of the Campaign to Save the Boundary Waters' amazing staff and volunteers. Levi Lexvold, our expedition manager, did an outstanding job keeping us well fed and supplied, and ensuring that as many people as possible could meet up with us throughout the year.

A special thanks to all the local "Wilderness Ninjas" Levi could call upon at a moment's notice to paddle in to pick up hard drives, or bring us resupplies when the conditions were dicey, and all of the people who paddled, hiked, dogsledded, snowshoed, and skied into the Wilderness to resupply us.

Thank you:
Paul and Sue Schurke for bringing in multiple resupplies by dog team and helping us stay warm all winter. Jane, Steve, and James Koschak, and Gail and Chris Bollis, for hosting and catering our entry and exit parties at River Point Resort. Reid Carron for helping with everything from grant applications to resupplies. Elton Brown for being our most frequent visitor. Steve Piragis, Willy Vosburgh, and Donna for your December resupply. Eric Frost, Jerry Vandiver, and Amberly Rosen for writing and recording "This Quiet Place." Nate Ptacek, Matty Van Biene, Kellen Witschen, and the crew at Duct Tape Then Beer, for filming and producing the short film, *Bear Witness*. Jason Zabokrtsky and the Goldsteins for resupplying us throughout the year. Lindsey Lang, Emily Brown, Laverne and Barb Dunsmore, Corie McKibben, Brad Carlson, Barbara Garza, Chris Chandler, Lukas Leaf, Bernard Herrmann, Dave Gossage, and everyone else who made us homemade goodies. Frank and Sherri Moe, Tina, Tank, and Acorn for adding so much joy to our time in the Wilderness. Chuck Zeugner for helping us do our taxes. Lynden and Lawson Gerdes, and Bert and Johnnie Hyde, for teaching us how to harvest wild rice. Nate Ptacek, Ellie Siler, Michelle Hesterberg, and Ron Doctor for

letting us include your images in the book. Ben Weaver for sharing your music and poems with us. The crew at Sawbill Outfitters for fixing our canoe and paddling out to greet us. The folks at WTIP for producing our weekly podcast. Jerritt Johnston for all your help with the Wilderness Classroom. Wende and Scott Nelson for the lovely house where we wrote most of this book.

We would also like to thank Daniel Slager from Milkweed Editions for helping us every step of the way, and Joey McGarvey, Annie Harvieux, and Mary Austin Speaker for helping us edit and lay out the book.

Finally, we would like to thank our parents for fostering our love of the outdoors, and all our family and friends who have bid us farewell and welcomed us home so many times. We have missed weddings, births, birthdays, surgeries, and funerals over the course of our endless wanderings. Thank you for always being there for us when we return.

milkweed
editions

Founded as a nonprofit organization in 1980, Milkweed
Editions is an independent publisher. Our mission is to
identify, nurture, and publish transformative literature,
and build an engaged community around it.

We are aided in this mission by generous individuals
who make a gift to underwrite books on our list.
Special underwriting for *A Year in the Wilderness*
was provided by the following supporters:

Christopher and Katherine Crosby

The Hlavka Family

Stephen and Cynthia Snyder

Eleanor and Fred Winston
*In memory of Larry Steiner and his dedication
to Milkweed Editions*

milkweed.org